£5.95

Ordnance Survey
Peak District
Walks

Pathfinder Guide

Compiled by Brian Conduit

D0307732

Key to colour coding

The walks are divided into three broad categories, indicated by the following colours:

Short, easy walks

Walks of moderate length, likely to involve some modest uphill walking

More challenging walks, which may be longer and/or over more rugged terrain, often with some stiff climbs

Acknowledgements

I would like to thank Mr R.S.G. Smith (Head of the National Park Information Services), Mr J.A. Greenwood (National Park Senior Information Officer) and the National Park Rangers, as well as Mr M.J.S. Turner (Regional Director of the National Trust) for looking at the manuscript and giving me much useful advice.

While every care has been taken to ensure the accuracy of the route directions, the publishers cannot accept responsibility for errors or omissions, or for changes in details given. It has to be emphasised that the countryside is not static: hedges and fences can be removed, field boundaries can alter, footpaths can be rerouted and changes of ownership can result in the closure or diversion of some concessionary paths. Also paths that are easy and pleasant for walking in fine conditions may become slippery, muddy and difficult in wet weather and stepping stones over rivers and streams may become impassable.

Ordnance Survey   ISBN 0-319-00179-2
Jarrold Publishing   ISBN 0-7117-0464-3

First published 1989 by Ordnance Survey and Jarrold Publishing
Reprinted 1990

Ordnance Survey   Jarrold Publishing
Romsey Road   Barrack Street
Maybush   Norwich NR3 1TR
Southampton SO9 4DH

© Crown copyright 1989

Printed in Great Britain by Jarrold Printing, Norwich. 2/90

Previous page: *Standedge, where the Peak District merges into the South Pennines*

Contents

Introduction to the Peak District

There are two popular misconceptions about the Peak District: one that, as its name suggests, it is a region of peaks, and the other that it is almost wholly within and virtually synonymous with Derbyshire.

If the usual definition of a peak as a high, rather sharp-looking summit is accepted, there are none to be found here. The few hills that rise to over 2,000 feet, Kinder Scout and Bleaklow, are somewhat featureless and flat-topped, and those that do have a pointed, 'peak-like' appearance, such as Shutlingsloe and Win Hill, are considerably lower. The region was first called 'Peac-land' in Anglo-Saxon times and the local tribe were referred to as Pecsaetan or peak-dwellers. It is likely that the name comes from the Old English word *peac* meaning hill, i.e. hilly district, later altered to Peakland or simply the Peak.

Shutlingsloe's distinctive shape earns for it the nickname of 'the Cheshire Matterhorn', evidence that the Peak District is not confined to Derbyshire. Although the heart of the region lies in that county, a substantial proportion of it spills over into neighbouring Staffordshire, Cheshire, Greater Manchester, South Yorkshire and West Yorkshire. Indeed the Peak District, twice as long as it is broad, stretches almost from Huddersfield in the north (as typical a Pennine mill town as one could find) to the outskirts of Derby in the south, which unmistakably belongs to the industrial belt of the Midland plain; not only covering a considerable distance but also, in the course of the journey, crossing an obvious physical, historical and cultural frontier.

The frontier theme is an important and constantly recurring one. The Peak District is situated in the heart of England, at the crossroads between the 'highlands' and the 'lowlands'. Its southern flanks overlook – sweeping in a wide arc from west to east – the Cheshire plain and the gently rolling country of the vale of Trent and its tributaries. In contrast, the north of the region belongs firmly to northern England and surveys the bare and open Pennine moorlands, whose valleys are occupied by the tightly-packed industrial communities of Greater Manchester on one side and West and South Yorkshire on the other, a totally different scene.

This duality is reflected in the scenery. Within a comparatively small area, a walker can take his choice from the diversity of landscape offered by the 'White Peak' of the south and the 'Dark Peak' of the north. In the former he will explore a sweeping pastoral countryside of bright green fields, criss-crossed by miles of drystone walling, cut into by steep-sided wooded dales that provide some of the most spectacular riverside scenery in the country, dotted with idyllic villages. The rugged Dark Peak is equally appealing but in more challenging and less obvious ways. Here the lonely and empty moorlands seem to stretch for ever, and even the intrusion of man-made features, such as conifer plantations and reservoirs in some of the valleys, fails to dispel the feeling of wildness here, both forbidding and exhilarating.

Geology lies at the root of these scenic contrasts. The Peak District comprises a southern core of carboniferous limestone (the White Peak) and a northern core of gritstone (the Dark Peak), with two broad fingers of gritstone reaching down the western and eastern edges, almost enveloping the limestone in a semi-circle. The eastern finger forms one of the region's most striking features, the gritstone edges, an almost unbroken line of crags that extends for 12 miles along the eastern rim of the Derwent valley, providing not only superb views and excellent walking routes but also opportunities to try out rock climbing skills. The corresponding western finger is less continuous but produces the spectacular edges of Hen Cloud and the Roaches, overlooking the Staffordshire lowlands.

Gritstone, alternatively known as millstone grit because its hardness made it ideal for use in corn mills, dominates the northern Peak; a country of wild, bleak and windswept moorlands, whose thin soils, bereft of the tree cover they once had, can only support mosses,

The conical shape of Win Hill is a distinctive landmark

cotton grass, bilberries and heather. The latter makes a glorious sight in late summer and autumn, when it creates a carpet of pink and mauve. On the highest parts of these moors even this sparse vegetation disappears, leaving only the peat bogs, which are split into channels called 'groughs', which may be broad and steep-sided. To plod across such poorly drained and difficult terrain requires a combination of experience, stamina and a sense of humour; without these qualities such areas are to be avoided, especially in bad weather. Rising above these expanses are the gritstone tors, harder and more resistant rocks which have been fashioned by constant exposure to the weather into the most incredible and grotesque shapes. Not only do they break the monotony of the scene but they also act as useful landmarks for walkers in an otherwise featureless landscape. Some of the most spectacular of these are to be seen on the southern flanks of Kinder and along Derwent Edge, where it is easy to see why they have been given such nicknames as the Pagoda Rocks, the Wool Packs, the Cakes of Bread and the Coach and Horses.

The White Peak is basically a limestone plateau dissected by the valleys of the Manifold, the Dove, the Lathkill and the Wye, whose waters, swollen by torrents of melt-water from retreating glaciers during the Ice Age, cut through the rock to create almost perpendicular gorges. These gorges are edged with expanses of bare, gleaming white rock, while the more resistant limestones have remained as isolated hills or as thin pillars or needles, such as the spectacular series in Dovedale that includes Ilam Rock, Pickering Tor and Tissington Spires.

It is above all the porous quality of the rock that gives limestone scenery its most outstanding and distinctive characteristics. Water finds its way through joints in the rock and, absorbing carbon dioxide from the atmosphere, forms a weak acid solution which gradually dissolves it. This produces the twin phenomena of dry valleys on the surface and subterranean streams. Examples of totally dry valleys are Cave Dale and Winnat's Pass near Castleton. In the case of the Manifold and its tributary the Hamps, the rivers disappear and reappear, the Manifold vanishing through swallow or shake holes below Thor's Cave near Wetton, leaving a dry river-bed (except in wet weather) and bubbling up to the surface again about 5 miles downstream near Ilam. As the underground streams penetrate, they continue to dissolve the limestone, creating caves with stalactites and stalagmites. The most spectacular and most visited series of caves, some natural and some the result of lead-workings, are those just outside Castleton, but there are others near Buxton (Poole's Cavern) and around Matlock.

On the borders between the White and Dark Peak are shales, silts and sandstones compressed together in layers. These rocks, being less resistant than gritstone, are more friable and unstable, and sometimes produce landslips. Mam Tor, nicknamed the 'Shivering Mountain' because of its instability, has had several landslips, one of which led to the closure of the A625, which ran below it, and a particularly large landslip produced the dramatic outline of Alport Castles, so called because its shape resembles a medieval fortress.

Despite its central location, the Peak District has been a backwater throughout most of its history, isolated from the mainstream of national life, at least until the Industrial Revolution. There are some prehistoric remains, notably the stone circles at Arbor Low and Nine Ladies Circle on Stanton Moor, and some hill forts. The Romans made little impact; apart from sampling the spa waters at Buxton, their main interest in the area seems to have been the lead-mines. They built two forts, one at Brough in the Hope Valley and the other near Glossop, linked by a road, most of which follows the line of the present A57 (Snake Pass), but some parts take to the open moors and make a superb footpath, called Doctor's Gate after a sixteenth-century vicar of Glossop.

The history of the Dark Ages following the withdrawal of the Romans is obscure, and particularly so in the case of the Peak District. All that can be said is that the area was penetrated by Anglo-Saxons and later by Danes, and that as it was on the borders between the kingdoms of Mercia and Northumbria and likely to have been a source of conflict the frontier theme reappears. The 'Battle Stone' near Ilam is supposed to commemorate a battle between Anglo-Saxons and Vikings; apart from this the major physical evidence surviving from that period are the crosses at Hope, Eyam, Ilam and elsewhere.

The Norman kings converted much of the region into a hunting ground, the Royal Forest of the Peak, with its own special laws and administration. The forest was governed from Peveril Castle,

Nine Ladies stone circle lies in a woodland clearing

built by William Peverel, illegitimate son of William the Conqueror and Steward of the Forest, whose impressive and substantial ruins still tower above Castleton – the 'castle town' that grew up beneath its protective walls, but which never attained any size or importance. The only real town within the Peak District at this time was Bakewell, an important route and trading centre.

Out of the proceeds of sheep-farming and lead-mining, the mainstays of the medieval Peakland economy, a number of villages grew into small market towns and were granted charters. Many of these were more important then than they are today and their prosperity is reflected in the size and splendour of their churches, especially at Tideswell, where the aptly named 'Cathedral of the Peak' looks out of proportion to the modest town over which it presides.

Wealth generated from sheep-farming and lead-mining not only produced expanded villages and fine churches but also enabled local landowning families to build mansions for themselves. One of the most perfect and unspoilt medieval manor houses in the country is Haddon Hall, one of the homes of the dukes of Rutland. Most splendid and palatial of all the great houses in the Peak District is Chatsworth, standing amidst formal gardens and magnificently landscaped parkland, an expression of the power and wealth of the dukes of Devonshire, the first of whom rebuilt the Tudor house in the late seventeenth and early eighteenth centuries. Echoing the classical dignity of Chatsworth is Lyme Hall, on the north-western fringe of the Peak, literally not a stone's throw from urban Greater Manchester, standing in more rugged and informal parkland originally carved from Macclesfield Forest.The expansion and growing prosperity of farming is also reflected in the building or rebuilding of scores of humbler manor and farm houses throughout the area between the sixteenth and eighteenth centuries, while the construction of miles of drystone walls, admired as one of the most conspicuous if least pretentious of the man-made features of the White Peak, illustrates the growth of the enclosure movement, mainly during the eighteenth and early nineteenth centuries.

Quarrying expanded and both lead- and copper-mining reached their zenith during the eighteenth century. It was also at this time that the Peak District's isolation began to break down. Two widely disparate figures who played major roles in this process were the fifth Duke of Devonshire and Sir Richard Arkwright. The former attempted to turn Buxton into a northern equivalent of Bath, using some of his copper-mining profits to build the elegant Crescent, on the lines of Bath's Royal Crescent. The latter made the Peak District one of the 'cradles of the Industrial Revolution', when he moved from Lancashire and set up his cotton mill at Cromford, utilising the water power of the Derwent.

Although Buxton did not become another Bath and Cromford did not grow into another Bolton or Blackburn, the pioneering efforts of both men did lead to important changes in the nineteenth century. The eleventh Duke of Norfolk developed Glossop as a textile town, an outlier of the Lancashire cotton belt. Communications, which had hitherto been limited mostly to pack-horse trails, improved. Roads and railways brought visitors into the region, the start of mass tourism. First came the upper and middle classes to take the waters and view the 'wonders of nature', followed by workers from the nearby overcrowded industrial towns. Buxton (near Manchester and Stockport) and Castleton (convenient for Sheffield) became popular venues, but the most popular of all was Matlock Bath in the south, close to Stoke-on-Trent, Derby and Nottingham, which, with its combination of spa waters, caves, boating, gardens and riverside walks, became a mixture of Buxton and Blackpool.

The twentieth century has brought major changes to the landscape of parts of the Dark Peak, both through the planting of large blocks of conifers and the construction of reservoirs, especially in the Goyt and Upper Derwent valleys, Longdendale, Saddleworth and Wessenden Moors and the Bradfield area west of Sheffield, in order to satisfy the

Timeless tranquillity at Tissington

needs of the surrounding industrial towns. But in the present century the Peak District has met the needs of the nearby industrial areas in another important way – as a lung, a vital recreational outlet.

Unique amongst the National Parks, the Peak District is surrounded by heavily populated and highly industrialised areas. Among the towns that lie within its orbit are Stockport, Manchester, Oldham, Rochdale, Huddersfield, Barnsley, Sheffield, Chesterfield, Mansfield, Nottingham, Derby and Stoke-on-Trent. These, together with their adjoining areas, make up a sizeable proportion of the total population of England. No wonder that the Peak District became the main battleground of the 'access to the countryside' movement in the 1920s and 1930s when, for the population of those towns, it was the nearest piece of open and unspoilt country where, on one day of the week

at least, they could stretch their legs and breathe fresh air.

No wonder also that in 1951 it became the first of Britain's National Parks. Since then, not only has the National Park Authority protected and enhanced both its natural beauty and its extensive footpath network, it has also added to its recreational assets by making access agreements to open up areas of high moorland to the more adventurous rambler and taking over stretches of disused railway track and converting them into footpaths and bridle-ways, suitable for elderly, the less fit and even disabled walkers.

These two very different kinds of footpath illustrate the many and varied attractions of the Peak District as a walking area. There is something for everyone here – from tough and exhausting high moorland treks to gentle riverside strolls through delightful dales.

The National Parks and countryside recreation

Ten National Parks were created in England and Wales as a result of an Act of Parliament in 1949. In addition to these, there are numerous specially designated Areas of Outstanding Natural Beauty, Country and Regional Parks, Sites of Special Scientific Interest and picnic areas scattered throughout England, Wales and Scotland, all of which share the twin aims of preservation of the countryside and public accessibility and enjoyment.

In trying to define a National Park, one point to bear in mind is that unlike many overseas ones, Britain's National Parks are not owned by the nation. The vast bulk of the land in them is under private ownership. John Dower, whose report in 1945 created their framework, defined a National Park as 'an extensive area of beautiful and relatively wild country in which, for the nation's benefit and by appropriate national decision and action, (a) the characteristic landscape beauty is strictly preserved, (b) access and facilities for public open-air enjoyment are amply provided, (c) wildlife and buildings and places of architectural and historic interest are suitably protected, while (d) established farming use is effectively maintained'.

The concept of having designated areas of protected countryside grew out of a number of factors that appeared towards the end of the nineteenth century; principally greater facilities and opportunities for travel, the development of various conservationist bodies and the establishment of National Parks abroad. Apart from a few of the early individual travellers such as Celia Fiennes and Daniel Defoe, who were usually more concerned with commenting on agricultural improvements, the appearance of towns and the extent of antiquities to be found than with the wonders of nature, interest in the countryside as a source of beauty, spiritual refreshment and recreation, and, along with that, an interest in conserving it, did not arise until the Victorian era. Towards the end of the eighteenth century, improvements in road transport enabled the wealthy to visit regions that had hitherto been largely inaccessible and, by the middle of the nineteenth century, the construction of the railways opened up such possibilities to the middle classes and, later on, to the working classes in even greater numbers. At the same time, the Romantic movement was in full swing and, encouraged by the works of Wordsworth, Coleridge and Shelley, interest and enthusiasm for wild places, including the mountain, moorland and hill regions of northern and western Britain, were now in vogue. Eighteenth-century taste had thought of the Scottish Highlands, the Lake District and Snowdonia as places to avoid, preferring controlled order and symmetry in nature as well as in architecture and town planning. But upper and middle class Victorian travellers were thrilled and awed by what they saw as the untamed savagery and wilderness of mountain peaks, deep and secluded gorges, thundering waterfalls, towering cliffs and rocky crags. In addition, there was a growing reaction against the materialism and squalor of Victorian industrialisation and urbanisation and a desire to escape from the formality and artificiality of town life into areas of unspoilt natural beauty.

A result of this was the formation of a number of different societies, all concerned with the 'great outdoors': naturalist groups, rambling clubs and conservationist organisations. One of the earliest of these was the Commons, Open Spaces and Footpaths Preservation Society, originally founded in 1865 to preserve commons and develop public access to the countryside. Particularly influential was the National Trust, set up in 1895 to protect and maintain both places of natural beauty and places of historic interest, and, later on, the Councils for the Preservation of Rural England, Wales and Scotland, three separate bodies that came into being between 1926 and 1928.

The world's first National Park was the Yellowstone Park in the United States, designated in 1872. This was followed by others in Canada, South Africa, Germany, Switzerland, New

Zealand and elsewhere, but in Britain such places did not come about until after the Second World War. Proposals for the creation of areas of protected countryside were made before the First World War and during the 1920s and 1930s, but nothing was done. The growing demand from people in towns for access to open country and the reluctance of landowners — particularly those who owned large expanses of uncultivated moorland — to grant it led to a number of ugly incidents, in particular the mass trespass in the Peak District in 1932, when fighting took place between ramblers and game-keepers and some of the trespassers received stiff prison sentences.

It was in the climate exemplified by the Beveridge Report and the subsequent creation of the welfare state, however, that calls for country-side conservation and access came to fruition in parliament. Based on the recommendations of the Dower Report (1945) and the Hobhouse Committee (1947), the National Parks and Country-side Act of 1949 provided for the designation and preservation of areas both of great scenic beauty and of particular wildlife and scientific interest throughout Britain. More specifically it provided for the creation of National Parks in England and Wales. Scotland was excluded because, with greater areas of open space and a smaller population, there were fewer pressures on the Scottish countryside and there-fore there was felt to be less need for the creation of such protected areas.

A National Parks Commission was set up, and over the next eight years ten areas were designated as parks; seven in England (Northumberland, Lake District, North York Moors, Yorkshire Dales, Peak District, Exmoor and Dartmoor) and three in Wales (Snowdonia, Brecon Beacons and Pembrokeshire Coast). At the same time the Commission was also given the responsibility for designating other smaller areas of high recreational and scenic qualities (Areas of Outstanding Natural Beauty), plus the power to propose and develop long-distance footpaths, now called National Trails,

though it was not until 1965 that the first of these, the Pennine Way, came into existence.

Further changes came with the Countryside Act of 1968 (a similar one for Scotland had been passed in 1967). The National Parks Commission was replaced by the Countryside Commis-sion, which was now to oversee and review virtually all aspects of country-side conservation, access and provision of recreational amenities. The Country Parks, which were smaller areas of countryside often close to urban areas, came into being. A number of long-distance footpaths were created, followed by an even greater number of unofficial long- or middle-distance paths, devised by individuals, ramblers' groups or local authorities. Provision of car parks and visitor centres, way-marking of public rights of way and the production of leaflets giving suggestions for walking routes all increased, a reflection both of increased leisure and of a greater desire for recreational activity, of which walking in particular, now recognised as the most popular leisure pursuit, has had a great explosion of interest.

The authorities who administer the individual National Parks have the very difficult task of reconciling the interests of the people who live and earn their living within them with those of the visitors. National Parks, and the other designated areas, are not living museums. Developments of various kinds, in housing, transport and rural industries, are needed. There is pressure to exploit the resources of the area, through more intensive farming, or through increased quarrying and forestry, extraction of minerals or the construction of reservoirs.

In the end it all comes down to a question of balance; a balance between conservation and 'sensitive develop-ment'. On the one hand there is a responsibility to preserve and enhance the natural beauty of the National Parks and to promote their enjoyment by the public, and on the other, the needs and well-being of the people living and working in them have to be borne in mind.

The National Trust

Anyone who likes visiting places of natural beauty and/or historic interest has cause to be grateful to the National Trust. Without it, many such places would probably have vanished by now, either under an avalanche of concrete and bricks and mortar or through reservoir construction or blanket afforestation.

It was in response to the pressures on the countryside posed by the relentless march of Victorian industrialisation that the Trust was set up in 1895. Its founders, inspired by the common goals of protecting and conserving Britain's national heritage and widening public access to it, were Sir Robert Hunter, Octavia Hill and Canon Rawnsley; a solicitor, a social reformer and a clergyman respectively. The latter was particularly influential. As a canon of Carlisle Cathedral and vicar of Crosthwaite (near Keswick), he was concerned about threats to the Lake District and had already been active in protecting footpaths and promoting public access to open countryside. After the flooding of Thirlmere in 1879 to create a large reservoir, he and his two colleagues became increasingly convinced that the only effective protection was outright ownership of land.

The purpose of the National Trust is to preserve areas of natural beauty and sites of historic interest by acquisition, holding them in trust for the nation and making them available for public access and enjoyment. Some of its properties have been acquired through purchase, but many have been donated. Nowadays it is one of the biggest landowners in the country and protects over half a million acres of land, including nearly 500 miles of coastline and a large number of historic properties (mostly houses) in England, Wales and Northern Ireland. (There is a separate National Trust for Scotland, which was set up in 1931.)

Furthermore, once a piece of land has come under Trust ownership, it is difficult for its status to be altered. As a result of Parliamentary legislation in 1907, the Trust was given the right to declare its property inalienable, so ensuring that in any dispute it can appeal directly to Parliament.

As it works towards its dual aims of conserving areas of attractive countryside and encouraging greater public access (not easy to reconcile in this age of mass tourism), the Trust provides an excellent service to walkers by creating new concessionary paths and waymarked trails, by maintaining stiles and footbridges and by combating the ever increasing problem of footpath erosion.

The Ramblers' Association

No organisation works more actively to protect and extend the rights and interests of walkers in the countryside than the Ramblers' Association. Its aims (summarised here) are clear: to foster a greater knowledge, love and care of the countryside; to assist in the protection and enhancement of public rights of way and areas of natural beauty; to work for greater public access to the countryside and to encourage more people to take up rambling as a healthy, recreational activity.

It was founded in 1935 when, following the setting up of a National Council of Ramblers' Federation in 1931, a number of federations earlier formed in London, Manchester, the Midlands and elsewhere came together to create a more effective pressure group, to deal with such contemporary problems as the disappearance and obstruction of footpaths, the prevention of access to open mountain and moorland and increasing hostility from landowners. This was the era of the mass trespasses, when there were sometimes violent confrontations between ramblers and gamekeepers, especially on the moorlands of the Peak District.

Since then the Ramblers' Association has played an influential role in preserving and developing the national footpath network, supporting the creation of National Parks and encouraging the designation and waymarking of long-distance footpaths.

Our freedom to walk in the countryside is precarious, and requires constant vigilance. As well as the perennial problems of footpaths being illegally obstructed, disappearing through lack of use or extinguished by housing or road construction, new dangers can spring up at any time.

It is to meet such problems and dangers that the Ramblers' Association exists and represents the interests of all walkers. The address to write to for information on the Ramblers' Association and how to become a member is given on page 78.

Walkers and the law

The average walker in a National Park or other popular walking area, armed with the appropriate Ordnance Survey map, reinforced perhaps by a guidebook giving detailed walking instructions, is unlikely to run into legal difficulties, but it is useful to know something about the law relating to public rights of way. The right to walk over certain parts of the countryside has developed over a long period of time, and how such rights came into being and how far they are protected by the law is a complex subject, fascinating in its own right, but too lengthy to be discussed here. The following comments are intended simply to be a helpful guide, backed up by the Countryside Access Charter, a concise summary of walkers' rights and obligations drawn up by the Countryside Commission.

Basically there are two main kinds of public rights of way: footpaths (for walkers only) and bridle-ways (for walkers, riders on horseback and pedal cyclists). Footpaths and bridle-ways are shown by broken green lines on Ordnance Survey Pathfinder and Outdoor Leisure maps and broken red lines on Landranger maps. There is also a third category, called byways or 'roads used as a public path': chiefly broad, walled tracks (green lanes) or farm roads, which walkers, riders and cyclists have to share, usually only occasionally, with motor vehicles. Many of these public paths have been in existence for hundreds of years and some even originated as prehistoric trackways and have been in constant use for well over 2,000 years.

The term 'right of way' means exactly what it says. It gives right of passage over what, in the vast majority of cases, is private land, and you are required to keep to the line of the path and not stray onto the land either side. If you inadvertently wander off the right of way − either because of faulty map-reading or because the route is not clearly indicated on the ground − you are technically trespassing and the wisest course is to ask the nearest available person (farmer or fellow walker) to direct you back to the correct route. There are stories of unpleasant confrontations between walkers and farmers at times, but in general most farmers are helpful and co-operative when responding to a genuine and polite request for assistance in route finding.

Obstructions can sometimes be a problem and probably the commonest of these is where a path across a field has been ploughed up. It is legal for a farmer to plough up a path provided that he restores it within two weeks, barring exceptionally bad weather. This does not always happen and here the walker is presented with a dilemma. Does he follow the line of the path, even if this inevitably means treading on crops, or does he use his common sense and walk around the edge of the field? The latter course of action often seems the best but, as this means that you would be trespassing, you are, in law, supposed to keep to the exact line of the path, avoiding unnecessary damage to crops. In the case of other obstructions which may block a path (illegal fences and locked gates etc.), common sense again has to be used in order to negotiate them by the easiest method (detour or removal), followed by reporting the matter to the local council or National Park authority.

Apart from rights of way enshrined by law, there are a number of other paths available to walkers. Permissive or concessionary paths have been created where a landowner has given permission for the public to use a particular route across his land. The main problem with these is that, as they have been granted as a concession, there is no legal right to use them and therefore they can be extinguished at any time. In practice, many of these concessionary routes have been established on land owned either by large public bodies such as the Forestry Commission or the water authorities, or by a private one, such as the National Trust, and as these mainly encourage walkers to use their paths, they are unlikely to be closed unless a change of ownership occurs.

Walkers also have free access to Country Parks (except where requested to keep away from certain areas for ecological reasons e.g. wildlife protection, woodland regeneration, safeguarding of rare plants etc.), canal towpaths and most beaches. By custom, though not by right, you are generally free to walk across the open and uncultivated higher land of mountain, moorland and fell, but this varies from area to area and from one season to another − grouse moors, for example, will be out of bounds during the breeding and shooting seasons and some open areas are used as Ministry of Defence firing ranges, for which reason access will be restricted. In some areas the situation has been clarified as a result of 'access agreements' between the landowners and either the county council or the National Park authority, which clearly define when and where you can walk over such open country.

Countryside Access Charter

Your rights of way are:

- Public footpaths — on foot only. Sometimes waymarked in yellow
- Bridle-ways — on foot, horseback and pedal cycle. Sometimes waymarked in blue
- Byways (usually old roads), most 'roads used as public paths' and, of course, public roads — all traffic has the right of way.

Use maps, signs and waymarks to check rights of way. Ordnance Survey Pathfinder and Landranger maps show most public rights of way

On rights of way you can:

- take a pram, pushchair or wheelchair if practicable
- take a dog (on a lead or under close control)
- take a short route round an illegal obstruction or remove it sufficiently to get past

You have a right to go for recreation to:

- public parks and open spaces — on foot
- most commons near older towns and cities — on foot and sometimes on horseback
- private land where the owner has a formal agreement with the local authority

In addition you can use the following by local or established custom or consent, but ask for advice if you are unsure:

- many areas of open country, such as moorland, fell and coastal areas, especially those in the care of the National Trust, and some commons
- some woods and forests, especially those owned by the Forestry Commission
- Country Parks and picnic sites
- most beaches
- canal towpaths
- some private paths and tracks

Consent sometimes extends to horse-riding and cycling

For your information:

- county councils and London boroughs maintain and record rights of way, and register commons
- obstructions, dangerous animals, harassment and misleading signs on rights of way are illegal and you should report them to the county council
- paths across fields can be ploughed, but must normally be reinstated within two weeks
- landowners can require you to leave land to which you have no right of access
- motor vehicles are normally permitted only on roads, byways and some 'roads used as public paths'

The limestone splendour of Miller's Dale

Key Map 1

Key Map 2

CONVENTIONAL SIGNS 1:25 000 or 2½ INCHES to 1 MILE

ROADS AND PATHS

Not necessarily rights of way

M I or A 6(M)	M I or A 6(M)	Motorway
A 3 I (T)	A 3 I (T)	Trunk road
A 35	A 35	Main road
B 3074	B 3074	Secondary road
A 35	A 35	Dual carriageway

Narrow roads with passing places annotated

Road generally more than 4m wide

Road generally less than 4m wide

Other road, drive or track

Unfenced roads and tracks are shown by pecked lines

.... Path

RAILWAYS

	Multiple track	Standard gauge
	Single track	
	Narrow gauge	
	Siding	
	Cutting	
	Embankment	
	Tunnel	
	Road over & under	
	Level crossing; station	

PUBLIC RIGHTS OF WAY Public rights of way may not be evident on the ground

- - - - - - - - - } Public paths { Footpath
— — — — — }   { Bridleway

+ + + + + Byway open to all traffic
∔ ∔ ∔ ∔ Road used as a public path

The indication of a towpath in this book does not necessarily imply a public right of way
The representation of any other road, track or path is no evidence of the existence of a right of way

BOUNDARIES

— . — . — . — County (England and Wales)
— — — — — — District or
━╸◦━╸◦━╸◦━╸ London Borough
.... Civil Parish (England)* Community (Wales)
— — — — — — — Constituency (County, Borough, Burgh or European Assembly)

Coincident boundaries are shown by the first appropriate symbol

*For Ordnance Survey purposes County Boundary is deemed to be the limit of the parish structure whether or not a parish area adjoins

SYMBOLS

▋	Church	with tower
▋	or	with spire
+	chapel	without tower or spire
▨ ▲		Glasshouse; youth hostel
⬯		Bus or coach station
⚎ ⚎ ⌁		Lighthouse; lightship; beacon
△		Triangulation station
▋ ▋ ✣	Triangulation	church or chapel
⚎ ⚎	point on	lighthouse, beacon
▢ ⊙		building; chimney

Electricity
pylon pole transmission line

VILLA Roman antiquity (AD 43 to AD 420)
𝓒𝖆𝖘𝖙𝖑𝖊 Other antiquities
✚ Site of antiquity
⚔ 1066 Site of battle (with date)
  Gravel pit
  Sand pit
  Chalk pit, clay pit or quarry
  Refuse or slag heap
▬▬▬▬▬ Sloping wall

| ▢ | Water | ▢ | Mud |

Sand; sand & shingle

National Park or Forest Park Boundary

NT	National Trust always open
NT	National Trust opening restricted
FC	Forestry Commission

VEGETATION Limits of vegetation are defined by positioning of the symbols but may be delineated also by pecks or dots

Coniferous trees
Non-coniferous trees
Coppice
Orchard

Scrub
Bracken, rough grassland
In some areas bracken (⌃) and rough grassland (.......) are shown separately
Heath

Shown collectively as rough grassland on some sheets

Reeds
Marsh
Saltings

HEIGHTS AND ROCK FEATURES

| 50 · | Determined | ground survey |
| 285 · | by | air survey |

Surface heights are to the nearest metre above mean sea level. Heights shown close to a triangulation pillar refer to the station height at ground level and not necessarily to the summit

Vertical face

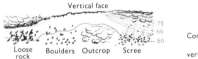

Loose rock   Boulders   Outcrop   Scree

Contours are at 5 metres vertical interval

ABBREVIATIONS 1:25 000 or 2½ INCHES to 1 MILE also 1:10 000/1:10 560 or 6 INCHES to 1 MILE

BP,BS	Boundary Post or Stone	P	Post Office	A,R	Telephone, AA or RAC
CH	Club House	Pol Sta	Police Station	TH	Town Hall
F V	Ferry Foot or Vehicle	PC	Public Convenience	Twr	Tower
FB	Foot Bridge	PH	Public House	W	Well
HO	House	Sch	School	Wd Pp	Wind Pump
MP,MS	Mile Post or Stone	Spr	Spring		
Mon	Monument	T	Telephone, public		

Abbreviations applicable only to 1:10 000/1:10 560 or 6 INCHES to 1 MILE

Ch	Church	GP	Guide Post	TCB	Telephone Call Box
F Sta	Fire Station	P	Pole or Post	TCP	Telephone Call Post
Fn	Fountain	S	Stone	Y	Youth Hostel

TOURIST INFORMATION

✝ Abbey, Cathedral, Priory

🐟 Aquarium

⋀ Camp site

⚏ Caravan site

🏰 Castle

📷 Cave

🎾 Country park

✄ Craft centre

🅿 Parking

PC Public Convenience (in rural areas)

𝔐 Ancient Monuments and Historic Buildings in the care of the Secretary

◆ Long Distance or Recreational Path

Pennine Way Named path

❀ Garden

⚑ Golf course or links

🏛 Historic house

ℹ Information centre

🏁 Motor racing

🖼 Museum

❗ Nature or forest trail

🐦 Nature reserve

☆ Other tourist feature

✕ Picnic site

🚂 Preserved railway

🏇 Racecourse

⛷ Skiing

❋ Viewpoint

🦌 Wildlife park

🐘 Zoo

𝕮𝖆𝖘𝖙𝖑𝖊 Selected places of interest
SAILING

✆ T Public telephone

⊕ Mountain rescue post

NATIONAL PARK Boundary of National Park access land
ACCESS LAND Private land for which the National Park Planning Board
have negotiated public access

◄ Access Point

WALKS

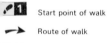 Start point of walk

➤ Route of walk

▬ Featured walk

FOLLOW THE COUNTRY CODE
Enjoy the countryside and respect its life and work

Guard against all risk of fire

Fasten all gates

Keep your dogs under close control

Keep to public paths across farmland

Leave livestock, crops and machinery alone

Use gates and stiles to cross fences, hedges and walls

Take your litter home

Help to keep all water clean

Protect wildlife, plants and trees

Take special care on country roads

Make no unnecessary noise

1 Bradfield Dale

Start:	Low Bradfield
Distance:	3 miles (4·75 km)
Approximate time:	1½ hours
Parking:	Car park by recreation ground in Low Bradfield
Refreshments:	Pub in Low Bradfield, pub in High Bradfield
Ordnance Survey maps:	Landranger 110 (Sheffield & Huddersfield) and Pathfinder 726 (Sheffield North and Stocksbridge)

General description *The bisected village of Bradfield is the focal point of this walk which, in a modest distance, manages to include a short but steep climb, areas of woodland, meadows, and fine views of rolling hills backed by the encircling moors, in a little-known part of the Peak District. It may come as a surprise to learn that the centre of Sheffield is only about seven miles away.*

The attractive village of Bradfield, sheltered by high moorlands, is divided into two distinct halves, ½ mile (0·8 km) apart and separated by a steep hill. Low Bradfield lies at the bottom near the head of the Loxley Valley and Bradfield Dale, and High Bradfield, dominated by the splendid church, occupies the top of the hill, 860 ft (258 m) high and commanding the most extensive views.

Start by turning right out of the car park and along the track beside it to a bridge. Do not cross the bridge but keep ahead along a narrow path (public footpath sign to High Bradfield) that squeezes between a wall on the left and a stream on the right to a second footbridge. This time turn right over the bridge, up a flight of steps, over a stone stile and bear left. Continue up a few more steps and keep ahead, between a fence and wall, to a road.

Turn left along the road for a short distance, by the edge of Agden Reservoir, one of four reservoirs in the area that supply some of Sheffield's water needs. Where the road curves to the right, turn right (**A**), at a public footpath sign to Bailey Hill, up more steps and along a winding uphill path by the right-hand side of a plantation. Climb steeply to a path junction by a stile on the right, and ahead is Bailey Hill, the site of a Norman motte and bailey castle, now partially overgrown with trees.

Turn right over the stile and along a path heading towards the church, passing through two gates and into the churchyard, from which the views down the dale are magnificent – a lovely patchwork of small fields, areas of woodland and expanses of water, with the moorlands stretching away on the horizon. Not only does the church occupy a superb position above the dale but it is also a very fine building in itself, unusually large and imposing for a small village and a superb example of Perpendicular architecture. Although dating chiefly from the fifteenth century, it possesses a fourteenth-century tower and a Celtic cross, which was placed in the church in 1886. The reason for the church's size and splendour is that it was built, endowed and staffed by the monks of nearby Ecclesfield Priory.

Walk through the churchyard and climb a stone stile by the side of a rather odd-looking Gothic house. This is the Watch House, built in 1745 in order that its occupants could deter body snatchers from plundering graves in the churchyard. Turn right and almost immediately left along Towngate, through High Bradfield, which contains a number of tall three-storeyed houses, the result of a domestic framework knitting industry which once flourished here – there are some similar

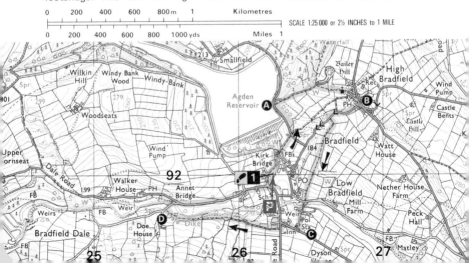

Bradfield Church, high above the dale

three-storeyed houses in Low Bradfield as well.

Turn right down Woodfall Lane **(B)**, signposted to Low Bradfield and Dungworth, and soon after the lane curves to the left, turn left at a public footpath sign to Low Bradfield, over a stone stile. Keep along the edge of a field by a wall on the left, following it as it curves to the right. Climb a stone stile, keep ahead to another one, climb that and, bearing slightly right away from a wall, make for the right-hand side of a fence and line of trees. Continue across a field, soon picking up a broken wall and keeping to the right of it downhill to a stone stile. Climb over and keep ahead to descend a flight of steps to a lane. Cross a footbridge almost opposite over the River Loxley, continue along a track and straight ahead along a walled path to a lane **(C)**.

Turn right to a junction by The Plough, turn left, and in a few yards turn right again, at a public footpath sign, along a walled track from where there are fine views all around of wooded hills, the rocks of Hurkling Edge on the right and Bradfield Church prominent on its hilltop site. Climb a stone stile and keep ahead, by the placid waters of Dale Dike on the right, to another stone stile. These waters have not always been so placid, for in 1864 the dam of Dale Dike Reservoir, a little further down the valley, was breached and the water

surged through the dale, devastating Low Bradfield and killing over 200 people. Climb the stile and continue along a pleasant grassy path on a ledge above the wooded stream to climb another stone stile.

Turn right along the lane **(D)**, cross Annet Bridge and, at a junction of lanes, bear right. Walk along the quiet wooded lane for ½ mile (0·8 km), keeping ahead at a junction and proceeding downhill into Low Bradfield. Where the lane starts to curve right, turn left along The Sands, soon bearing right back to the car park.

Rolling countryside around Bradfield

2 Glossop

Start:	Glossop
Distance:	3½ miles (5·5 km)
Approximate time:	2 hours
Parking:	Glossop town centre
Refreshments:	Pubs and cafés in Glossop
Ordnance Survey maps:	Landranger 110 (Sheffield & Huddersfield) and Outdoor Leisure 1 (The Peak District – Dark Peak area)

General description *The sombre moorlands of Kinder, Bleaklow and Saddleworth cradle the town of Glossop and this short and easy walk on its northern and eastern fringes, although not venturing onto these, gives fine views of them. It also reveals something of the industrial history of this part of the Peak District, where a combination of swift-flowing streams and proximity to Manchester enabled Glossop to become a cotton manufacturing town. Despite this, it is remarkably easy to get out into open country from the town centre, and Old Glossop, the original settlement now engulfed by the town but still retaining its separate identity, is a reminder of pre-Industrial Revolution days.*

In many ways Glossop, on the north-western fringes of the Peak District and near the industrial towns of Greater Manchester, is an extension of Lancashire. It was mainly the creation of the eleventh Duke of Norfolk, who developed it as a mill town in the early nineteenth century, and it possesses some fine Victorian public buildings including inevitably some impressive mills.

Start in the town centre and walk along the A57 towards Sheffield, turning left into Ellison Street. About 50 yards (46 m) up on the right is a footpath sign for Quarry Close, Smithy Close, Drovers Walk and King Edward Avenue. Turn right here along a path through a modern housing estate, passing school buildings on the left, and where the boundary fence of the school bends to the left, keep straight ahead. From here there is a good view on the right of both Kinder and Bleaklow. Pass close to a pool on the right, and at a junction of paths take the left-hand fork, continuing through trees and ahead between walls on both sides to a road **(A)**. Turn right into Old Glossop, soon leaving the road and keeping straight ahead along Church Walk, past the church, and turning right on rejoining the road. Although surrounded by newer, urban Glossop, Old Glossop manages to retain a real village atmosphere, with a number of attractive seventeenth-century cottages close to the church.

Glossop and its encircling moors

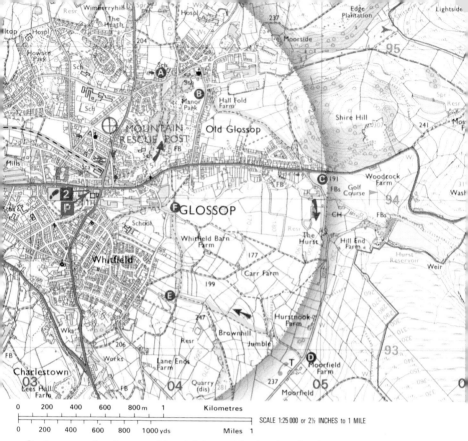

SCALE 1:25 000 or 2½ INCHES to 1 MILE

Continue over the stream and turn left by the side of the post office along Manor Park View **(B)**. Turn sharp right between barns and cottages and follow a walled track ahead. Look out for a gate and gap in the wall on the right, go through, keep ahead a few yards to another gap in a wall, pass through that and walk along the path ahead, from where there are impressive views over Glossop, situated in its valley and encircled by moorlands. Bear right through another wall gap, left along the edge of a playing field, and at the end of the field bear slightly left to take a narrow path along the backs of houses down to the main road **(C)**.

Cross over and take the lane opposite, passing a golf course on the left, go over a stream and keep ahead, now climbing gently but steadily. Continue over the brow of the hill, down the other side and, where the lane starts to curve gently to the right, turn right along a broad track by a group of trees **(D)**, heading towards a farm. At the farm buildings turn sharp left, almost doubling back, and turn right through a gate at the end of the buildings. Keep ahead for a few yards, turn left through a gate in a wall, and then turn right to follow the wall and fence round to the right to a stile.

Do not climb this stile but turn left and follow the edge of the field, by a fence on the right, keeping ahead at the end of the fence and climbing gently over Brown Hill to the corner of a wall. Keep ahead across the grass (no definite path) to a gate in the top left-hand corner of the field, go through and head diagonally across the next field, making for a gap in the wall at the far end. Pass through and continue straight across the middle of a long narrow field to a gate. Do not go through it but turn right **(E)** and, keeping by a wall on the left, pass through a gap in the wall in front and head downhill along the edge of a field. As you descend there are particularly fine views of Glossop below in the valley, Old Glossop church spire behind, the wooded Shire Hill to the right and, beyond, the bare moorlands of Bleaklow.

Climb a stile, cross a green lane, go through a gate opposite and continue downhill, through several more gates and over stone stiles, keeping by a wall on the left all the time, to a stile by a public footpath sign **(F)**. Turn left and follow the lane downhill between cottages, turning left at a public footpath sign along a path by a stream and mill on the right. The path, surprisingly rural considering how close it is to Glossop town centre, leads to a road. Here turn right along to the main road and turn right again back to the town centre.

3 Stanton Moor

Start:	Birchover
Distance:	3½ miles (5·5 km)
Approximate time:	2 hours
Parking:	Park at lower end of village street, or use parking area just above village and start the walk where path joins Stanton-in-Peak road. Drive through village, take road to Stanton-in-Peak and parking area is on the left at the top of the hill, just after sharp left and right bends
Refreshments:	Pubs in Birchover
Ordnance Survey maps:	Landranger 119 (Buxton, Matlock & Dovedale) and Outdoor Leisure 24 (The Peak District – White Peak area)

General description *Stanton Moor, an oasis of gritstone amidst limestone country, rises to 1,096 ft; an area of open, breezy, heather-clad moorland giving glorious views across the valley of the Derwent. Its two chief characteristics, which form the main features of this short walk, are the curious rock formations and the vast number of prehistoric remains – burial chambers, standing stones, circles and fortifications – which litter the moor.*

Birchover is a small village strung out along the hill that climbs up to Stanton Moor. At its lower end, just below the Druid Inn, a path on the right leads up to the Rowtor Rocks, a gritstone outcrop worth exploring both for its extensive views and for its maze of caves and passages, where carved steps lead to terraces at different levels. Many of these were the work of Thomas Eyre, an eccentric eighteenth-century clergyman, and just below the rocks is the tiny village church he built.

The walk starts by the Druid Inn. With your back to the inn, look out for a gap in the wall on the opposite side of the road, go through it and follow a narrow path that heads up above the village, between trees and hedges, to a road by a parking area. (Start the walk here if using this parking area.)

Turn left, walk along the road for ¼ mile (0·4 km) and, just after passing the group of large boulders on the right by the entrance to Stanton Park Quarry, turn right up to a stile a few yards ahead (**A**). Climb over and head across Stanton Moor, passing on the left the Cork Stone, an isolated standing stone beside a disused shallow quarry. Continue to a crossroads of paths and turn left across open moorland, with fine views to the right over the Derwent valley. All around are various prehistoric remains. Keep ahead to enter Stanton Moor Plantation, and Nine Ladies stone circle, the major prehistoric site on the moor, is soon reached a few yards to the left off the main path in a woodland clearing. This circle is thought to date from the Bronze Age and was probably erected around 1500 BC. Like all such circles, nothing substantial is known about it but it presumably had some religious significance.

Continue for a short distance through the trees and look out for a path on the right (**B**) leading down to a stile. Climb over and walk along the edge of the moor, beside a wire fence on the right and by more stones, and passing close to the Reform Tower, erected in honour of Earl Grey, of Reform Bill (and blend of tea) fame. At a particularly large stone, the Cat Stone, the path turns sharp right and then left, continuing ahead past more large stones to drop down to a lane (**C**).

Turn right along the lane for 200 yards (184 m) and, at a public footpath sign, turn left over a stone stile and head down towards a farm. Keeping to the left of the farm buildings, go through the farmyard, turn right at a public footpath sign (**D**) and, a few yards ahead, right at the next signpost. Climb a stone stile and keep ahead, bearing slightly to the left to meet a broad track which heads down to rejoin the lane. Bear left and follow the lane through Birchover, back to the Druid Inn at the bottom end of the village.

SCALE: 1:25 000 or 2½ INCHES to 1 MILE

4 Buxton Country Park

Start:	Buxton Country Park (Poole's Cavern)
Distance:	4½ miles (7 km)
Approximate time:	2½ hours
Parking:	Buxton Country Park
Refreshments:	None on the walk but plenty of pubs, restaurants and cafés in nearby Buxton
Ordnance Survey maps:	Landranger 119 (Buxton, Matlock & Dovedale) and Outdoor Leisure 24 (The Peak District – White Peak area)

General description *Here is a walk, on the southern fringes of Buxton, that shows how a once ravaged landscape can be restored to both beauty and usefulness. Buxton Country Park is based upon Grin Low Woods, originally planted in the early nineteenth century by one of the dukes of Devonshire, to hide ugly waste tips caused by centuries of quarrying and lime-burning, and also Grin Quarry, reclaimed and landscaped as a caravan site as recently as 1982. The two other major features are the great show cave of Poole's Cavern, which can be visited at the end of the walk, and Solomon's Temple, a nineteenth-century folly and fine viewpoint. This short walk leaves plenty of time not only to visit Poole's Cavern but also to explore the urban delights of nearby Buxton.*

Buxton is the Peak District's answer to Bath or Cheltenham, an elegant spa town of fine buildings ranging from Georgian to Edwardian times, the heyday of the spa. Chief amongst them are the eighteenth-century Crescent, the Devonshire Hospital, the Regency church, the Victorian Pavilion (overlooking beautiful gardens) and the opulent Edwardian Opera House, recently restored to its full splendour. Just to the south of the town is Poole's Cavern, an impressive natural cave named after an alleged medieval outlaw, which has yielded Roman items.

With your back to the road, turn left through a gate at the side of the car park, and go a short distance along a path to the road. Turn right for just over 100 yards (92 m) and, where the road curves left **(A)**, keep straight ahead across a field below the slopes of Grin Low Woods on the right. Climb a stile and continue ahead towards a line of houses.

At a fork in the paths by a group of trees on the left, take the right-hand fork, keeping by a low wall and wire fence on the right, and where both curve sharply to the right, keep straight ahead towards a broad tarmac track running parallel to the backs of the houses in front. Bear right along this track, go over a cattle grid and immediately turn right by a wall to a stone stile. Climb over and turn left along the edge of a field, by a wall on the left, along a very pleasant path amidst meadows and wooded hillsides. Soon the view ahead is dominated by the face of one of the numerous disused quarries in the Buxton area.

Passing a farm on the left, climb a stile by the end of the buildings and continue along a

Solomon's Temple – folly and fine viewpoint above Buxton

SCALE 1:25 000 or 2½ INCHES to 1 MILE

walled path for a few yards to a gate. Go through and keep along the edge of a field, climbing gently by woods on the left. Continue straight ahead past the end of the woods across fields, heading for a stile at a wall corner. Climb over and continue straight across a field, down to a stone stile and footpath sign, and onto a road **(B)**.

Turn left for a few yards and then turn sharp right at a public footpath sign, over a stile by a metal gate and along a track which winds uphill to a farm. Walk through the farmyard and continue along the track, which bears right and gives superb views of the long bare ridge of Axe Edge in front, and to the right Stanley Moor with Solomon's Temple conspicuous on the skyline. Follow the track down into a dip, then up again, curving first right, then left, and bearing right again, to join the boundary wall of Stanley Moor Reservoir with its surrounding trees. Continue ahead to a road **(C)**.

Here cross straight over to enter the Grin Low picnic site and car park, go through a gate and walk along the tarmac road ahead, across a grassy area reclaimed and landscaped from old quarry workings. Continue along the edge of the large quarry itself, which has now been converted into an attractive caravan and camp site, completed for the Caravan Club of Great Britain in 1981–82. Walk through the car park and along a well surfaced path, heading up the hill towards Solomon's Temple. Following signposts, turn left, then turn right through a gate, keep by the side of Grin Low Woods on the left, and head straight up to the temple on top of the hill in front **(D)**. Solomon's Temple, or Grinlow Tower as it is sometimes called, is a folly, built in 1896 by a local man called Solomon Mycock in order to provide work for the unemployed. The summit of the hill on which it stands is 1,440 ft (432 m) high; add to that the height of the tower, 25 ft, and it is not surprising that the views from the top are extensive and spectacular, with the buildings of Buxton immediately below and both Mam Tor and Kinder Scout visible on the horizon.

Now head downhill in the direction of the town to a wall. Climb a stone stile, and keep ahead across uneven ground (the result of former waste tips), turning left just before a broken wall towards a metal gate and stone stile. Climb the stile to enter Grin Low Woods, a most attractive area of 100 acres of native woodland, planted by one of the dukes of Devonshire in 1820 to hide what was a large and ugly waste tip – an early and most welcome example of successful landscape reclamation. Keep ahead, ignoring all paths to right and left, as far as a T-junction of paths. Here turn right along the main path that heads through the woods, finally turning right down some steps back to the car park by the entrance to Poole's Cavern.

5 Longshaw and Padley Gorge

Start:	Longshaw Country Park
Distance:	4 ½ miles (7 km)
Approximate time:	2 ½ hours
Parking:	Longshaw Country Park
Refreshments:	Longshaw Lodge Visitor Centre, Grindleford Station
Ordnance Survey maps:	Landranger 119 (Buxton, Matlock & Dovedale) and Outdoor Leisure 24 (The Peak District – White Peak area)

General description *A combination of open parkland and moorland, dense woodland and a beautiful steep-sided gorge makes for a walk of great scenic variety. Add to that the historic interest of a nineteenth-century hunting lodge and the remains of a fourteenth-century manor house, now converted into a chapel, plus fine panoramic views and well constructed National Trust paths throughout, and the result is not only a varied walk but one which, though undemanding and of modest length, is totally absorbing.*

Longshaw Country Park comprises 1,600 acres of woodland, grassland, farmland and moorland owned and maintained by the National Trust. It was formerly part of a much bigger estate of over 11,000 acres owned by the dukes of Rutland, which was sold and broken up in 1927. Fortunately the part of it adjacent to the lodge was bought by the Council for the Preservation of Rural England and Sheffield Council of Social Services, and later handed over to the National Trust, who have subsequently extended it to its present size.

From the car park take the path ahead to the National Trust information centre next to Longshaw Lodge. This palatial-looking building was put up in 1827 as a shooting lodge for the dukes of Rutland. After the sale of the estate it became a guest house; it is now divided into private flats. Cross a stream, and just before the lodge turn left along a woodland path that passes around the back of the lodge. Continue at first through most attractive woodland and then, after passing through a gate, across open grassland below a line of gritstone edges on the left. At a path junction bear left, following the slightly higher path to a road **(A)**.

Here bear right (bisecting the two roads on the right), go through a gate, at a National Trust sign for White Edge Moor, and along a track. After passing White Edge Lodge, the track becomes a grassy path that heads across the moor down to a road **(B)**. Cross over, turn left for a few yards and then turn sharp right through a gate, at a National Trust sign, and along a broad track.

At the first group of trees, turn left over a stile and follow a grassy path ahead into a shallow valley. Here turn right and, keeping by a stream on the left, drop down steeply, through the woodland that clothes the

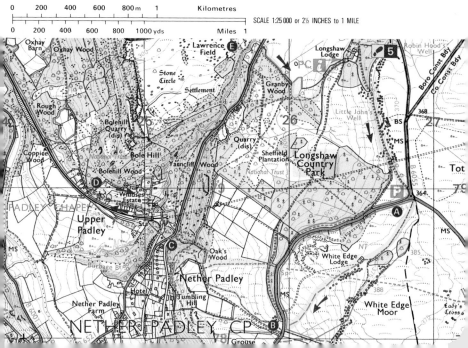

Burbage Brook rushes through wooded Padley Gorge

eastern slopes of Padley Gorge, to a road (C). Cross over, turn left for a few yards and then sharp right down through more woodland to Grindleford Station.

Cross the railway bridge and keep ahead over a stream to a path junction. Here keep straight ahead for just over ¼ mile (0·4 km), parallel with the railway line, to Padley Chapel (D). This was the gatehouse of a fourteenth-century manor house which, in Elizabeth I's reign, was owned by Sir Thomas Fitzherbert, a devout Catholic nobleman. In 1588, the year of the Spanish Armada, when rumours of Catholic plots were rife and when suspicion of English Catholics was at its greatest, two priests, who were caught hiding in the house, were arrested and sent to Derby where they were hanged, drawn and quartered. Sir Thomas was imprisoned and died in the Tower of London in 1591. The house fell into ruins and the gatehouse was even used as a cowshed until bought by the Roman Catholic diocese of Nottingham in 1933 and converted into a chapel.

Return to the path junction and turn left along a broad uphill track. After passing through a gate you enter the National Trust property of Padley Gorge, one of the few places in the Peak District where ancient woodland survives. The path continues through this beautiful wooded gorge, mainly keeping to the high ground above Burbage Brook on the right, which surges over the rocks in a series of small falls. Finally, after passing through a gate, you emerge from the wooded gorge and ahead is a superb view of Burbage Rocks.

Shortly afterwards turn right over a footbridge (E) and up to a gate that admits you to a road. Turn right along the road for a few yards, and turn left through a gate and along the edge of Granby Wood. Soon Longshaw Lodge can be seen to the left. The path skirts the edge of a pond and bears left across grassland, by trees and rhododendron bushes, back to Longshaw Lodge and the National Trust Information Centre. From here retrace your steps to the car park.

6 'Last of the Summer Wine'

Start:	Holmfirth
Distance:	5 miles (8 km)
Approximate time:	2½ hours
Parking:	Holmfirth
Refreshments:	Pubs and cafés in Holmfirth, pub in Upperthong, pub in Holmbridge
Ordnance Survey maps:	Landranger 110 (Sheffield & Huddersfield) and Pathfinder 714 (Holmfirth and Saddleworth Moor)

General description The countryside around Holmfirth is familiar to many as the setting for the popular television series Last of the Summer Wine. *This walk, of modest length but including a few short climbs, embraces farmland, woodland, rivers, some interesting old weaving villages and fine views of the encircling bowl of steep hills and rolling moors. On many of the paths and lanes you might at any moment expect to encounter a trio of adolescent pensioners, and if feeling the pangs of hunger and thirst you can always round off the walk by popping into Sid's Café.*

Two widely contrasting chance events have prevented Holmfirth from being just another typical Pennine woollen town on the north-eastern fringes of the Peak District. The first was the presence here of the enterprising James Bamforth who, having started with lantern slides and later flirted with film making before the First World War, concentrated on producing the famous saucy postcards, which have never changed and which still adorn gift and stationery shops at most seaside resorts. The second of course was that the town was chosen as the setting for the hugely successful television series, and this has attracted to it a new type of 'pilgrim', who comes here in order to see such modern 'shrines' as Nora Batty's house and Sid's Café. Away from these connections with the entertainment world, Holmfirth is an attractive town of narrow alleys, weavers' cottages and handsome old mills, and dominated by its eighteenth-century church.

Turn left out of the car park along the main street to traffic lights. In between the Tourist Information Centre and the Postcard Museum, turn right up some steps, and bearing right by a children's playground continue up more steps to a lane. Bear left up the lane and just to the right of the T-junction ahead is a public footpath sign. Turn left by the side of it up a narrow path, by a wall on the left, up more steps and past houses to another public footpath sign. Here turn left along a track **(A)** which immediately leaves the town behind and enters open country.

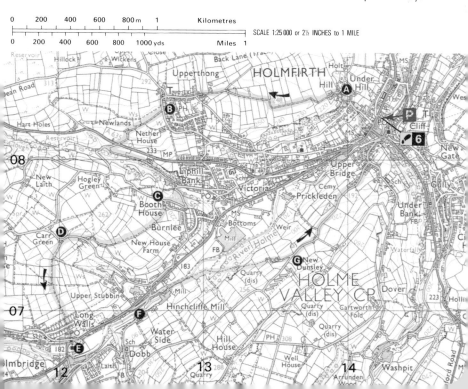

Holmfirth — on the Peak District's north-eastern fringes

Follow this twisting, walled track for one mile (1·5 km) to Upperthong, joining the road through the village called Towngate. Upperthong is one of a number of old weaving villages on the hills around Holmfirth where, before the advent of water-powered machinery, the families of farm workers augmented their wages by handloom weaving. It retains a number of attractive old weavers' cottages, characterised by their rows of mullioned windows.

Keep ahead at a road junction, soon bearing left downhill, and take the first turning on the right along another walled track **(B)**. Ahead are superb views of the Holme valley, backed by the sweeping moorlands of Wessenden Head Moor. Follow the track as it drops down to a road, keep straight ahead along a narrow lane opposite, and after 100 yards (92 m) turn left along another track above a stream on the right. This drops down through woodland to a lane by a junction. Turn sharp right, then turn left over a bridge and continue along an uphill lane which bends sharply to the right into the hamlet of Booth House, another old weaving community.

Turn first left **(C)**, bear left between houses, go up some steps ahead and continue for a few yards along a narrow path, by a wall on the right, to a stone stile. Climb over and continue across a field, soon joining a wall on the left. Keep by this wall for ½ mile (0·8 km), climbing two stiles and eventually continuing between cottages and tall three-storeyed houses to a lane.

Turn right and where the lane curves to the right turn sharp left **(D)**, at a public footpath sign, around the right-hand side of a house and down a walled track. Pass through a metal gate, keep ahead to squeeze through a gap in the right-hand corner of a wall a few yards ahead and continue by a wall on the left, downhill, passing through a succession of stiles, gaps and kissing-gates (even a metal turnstile), towards Holmbridge. At the last field before some houses, switch sides to follow a wall on the right, turn right through a gap at the bottom end of the field, and in a few yards turn left through a kissing-gate and down a path to a road through a housing estate. Cross the road and continue (between houses) down a path opposite to a lane, bearing left to reach the main road through Holmbridge **(E)**.

Bear left along the road for just under ½ mile (0·8 km), and at the first fork **(F)** keep straight ahead onto a side road. At the next junction continue along Water Street, passing a mill and heading down to the River Holme. Just past the mill, turn right over a footbridge and turn left along the other bank of the river to a stile. Climb over and continue across a field, bearing right away from the river and climbing slightly towards the trees ahead. Climb another stile in a wall to enter a wood, and take the path through the wood, heading uphill away from the wall on the left. By a small, half-hidden, disused quarry on the right, bear right off the main path, climbing up a narrower path to a stone stile in a wall. Climb over, bear left along a grassy path to another stone stile, climb that and continue to a farm. Climb another stile to the right of a gate, walk past the front of the farmhouse and keep ahead along a track between cottages to a lane **(G)**

Bear left along the lane and follow it for ½ mile (0·8 km) as it drops down into Holmfirth, giving grand views over the town and the surrounding hills and moors. At a T-junction, turn left downhill into the town centre opposite the church. Here you can either turn left over the river to traffic lights and then turn right to the car park, or follow pleasant paths by the river before turning left over a footbridge that leads directly into the car park.

7 Hope and Win Hill

Start:	Hope
Distance:	4 miles (6 km)
Approximate time:	2 hours
Parking:	Hope
Refreshments:	Pubs and cafés in Hope
Ordnance Survey maps:	Landranger 110 (Sheffield & Huddersfield) and Outdoor Leisure 1 (The Peak District – Dark Peak area)

General description *A short walk but one that involves a quite strenuous climb to the summit of Win Hill. The effort expended on the climb is rewarded with a superb panoramic view from the top followed by a pleasant and easy descent, through woods, across fields, past farms and finally by the little River Noe, and offering fine views over the Hope valley all the way.*

From the car park turn right along the main road, past the church, and turn first left along the road signposted to Edale. After ¼ mile (0·4 km), just before the road curves to the left, bear right **(A)** down to Killhill Bridge over the River Noe, cross it and continue along a tree-lined lane between high banks. Pass under the railway bridge and immediately turn sharp right, at a public footpath sign, along a broad track which soon turns left to begin the ascent of Win Hill, initially a gentle climb, but later becoming steeper.

Negotiate a kissing-gate, keep ahead to a farm, passing to the right of the farmhouse, and head up steeply across rough grass, making for a footpath sign by a gap in a wall ahead. Go through, follow the direction of the Win Hill sign to a ladder stile, climb that and continue climbing amongst heather, fern and gorse, enjoying the fine views to the right over the Hope valley. Soon the conical-shaped summit of Win Hill can be seen and

the path bears right towards it, joining a main path coming in from the left **(B)**. The views all round from the summit are magnificent and include Ladybower Reservoir, the Derwent Edges, Hope valley, the ridge stretching from Lose Hill to Mam Tor and beyond, and the brooding mass of Kinder.

From the summit continue ahead down to a pair of ladder stiles. Climb over and bear left into Winhill Plantation. At a fence, do not climb the stile ahead but turn right along a grassy path **(C)**, keeping by a wall on the right. Just where the path starts to descend between banks, turn right through a gap in that wall and bear left along a narrow but distinct grassy path that heads across open moorland, curving right around the end of a hill and dropping down to a ladder stile. Climb over and continue downhill across a field to a stile, climb that and keep ahead, by a wall on the right, to another stile. Climb that and continue along a walled path to a narrow lane **(D)**.

Here turn right through the hamlet of Aston, passing in front of Aston Hall. Keep along the lane for ½ mile (0·8 km), descending between steep, wooded banks, and at a public footpath sign to Killhill Bridge turn right along the drive of Farfield Farm **(E)**. Bear left at a yellow waymark in front of the farm buildings, and at the next waymark go through a gate and across a field, keeping to the right of two tall trees and making for a gate and stone stile in the far right-hand corner. Climb over, continue to a kissing-gate, pass through that, under the railway bridge and through another kissing-gate, and cross a field to the river. Here turn left along the tree-lined bank of the Noe up to some steps and onto the main road. Turn right along the road into Hope village.

SCALE: 1:25 000 or 2½ INCHES to 1 MILE

8 Lyme Park

Start:	Lyme Park
Distance:	5 miles (8 km)
Approximate time:	2½ hours
Parking:	Lyme Park
Refreshments:	Tea room at Lyme Hall
Ordnance Survey maps:	Landranger 109 (Manchester) and Pathfinder 741 (Stockport South)

General description The word 'park' usually conjures up an image of neat tarmacked paths, landscaped lawns, small areas of woodland and a lake, centered on a great house — all of which Lyme Park possesses. But within its boundaries there are also large areas of perhaps surprisingly rough and hilly grassland, and although this is only a short walk some fairly steep climbs are encountered. The park is located at the point where the Peak District meets both the Cheshire Plain and the built-up area of Greater Manchester (only six miles from the centre of Stockport), and the views from its highest points are both extensive and contrasting.

From the car park walk along the stepped path up to the entrance to the hall. For nearly 600 years Lyme Hall belonged to one family, the Leghs, but in 1946 Richard Legh, third Lord Newton, gave both the hall and the park to the National Trust, and it is now managed by Stockport Borough Council, to whom it was leased in 1947.

The north front, by which the hall is approached, is part of the original sixteenth-century mansion built by Sir Piers Legh, as are the drawing room and long gallery, the latter containing some superb Elizabethan oak panelling. Over the following three centuries the house was enlarged and reconstructed on several occasions, notably in the early eighteenth century by the Italian architect Leoni, and again in the early nineteenth century by Lewis Wyatt. Leoni's main contribution was the elegant classical south front, the most popular view of the hall, either from the gardens and pool or from the slopes of the surrounding hills a little further away. Inside, the house is a treasure store of fine paintings, furnishings and tapestries. Its formal gardens make a striking

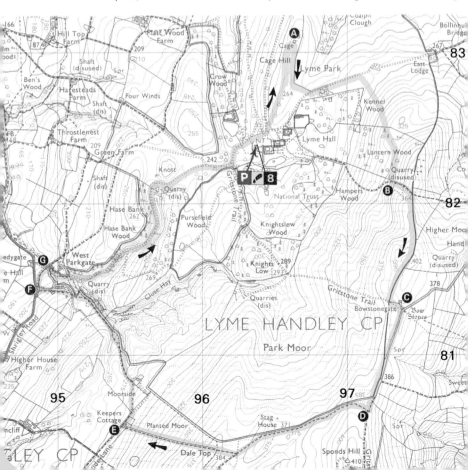

The classical elegance of Lyme Hall

contrast with the rough and open terrain of much of the walk.

The walk really commences by the entrance to the hall. With your back to the building, walk up the grassy slopes of the hill straight ahead to a prominent tower called the Cage. This was built in the sixteenth century as a viewing platform for the hunt, and partially reconstructed in the eighteenth century. The extensive scene from it today could hardly offer more of a contrast – the open and rugged moorlands of the Peak District to the south and the heavily urbanised and industrialised area of Greater Manchester to the north. Lyme Park was originally enclosed as a deer park, from the surrounding Macclesfield Forest, in 1346; it comprises over 1,300 acres of unspoilt grassland, woodland and moorland, and still possesses large numbers of deer.

Turn sharp right at the Cage (A), almost doubling back on your tracks, to follow a fence line as it curves left downhill to a drive. Turn left along this drive, then keep ahead along a path towards a circle of trees, and just before reaching the trees bear right and head uphill across rough grass, making for the edge of a wood near the brow of the hill. Climb over a ladder stile in the boundary wall of the wood and follow a path ahead through Lantern Wood, making a brief detour to the right to see the Lantern, a remnant of the Elizabethan hall later re-erected on this spot as a folly.

Continue through the wood, climb a ladder stile at the far end and turn left (B), keeping by the side of a wall, uphill, across rough, open grassland. Where two walls meet, bear right, now following the boundary wall of Lyme Park on the left, for just under ½ mile (0·8 km) to a ladder stile on the left. As you are now fairly high up on exposed moorland, there are extensive and uninterrupted views for the next mile (1·5 km), offering even more striking contrasts than those earlier – the foothills of the Peak District looking towards the brooding bulk of Kinder

Scout, the rolling hills of Macclesfield Forest dominated by the distinctive shape of Shutlingsloe, the flat farmlands of the Cheshire Plain punctuated by the abrupt ridge of Alderley Edge, the built-up area of Greater Manchester again and even distant glimpses of Merseyside.

Turn left over the ladder stile, walk along a grassy path to another stile and climb that to join a lane (C). A few yards to the left are the Bow Stones, the middle sections of a group of Anglo-Saxon crosses, the heads and bases being elsewhere. It is thought that they might have been placed here as boundary markers some time in the sixteenth century.

The route continues by turning right over a stile and along a wide track which gradually draws closer to the park wall on the right. After climbing the next stile, turn right (D) (here the park wall also does a right-hand turn), go over another stile and continue by the wall on the right. Keep by the wall for about ½ mile (0·8 km) and, on approaching a wire fence in front, bear slightly left away from it to climb a stile. Now head downhill, by a broken wall on the right, to reach a track called Moorside Lane (E).

Turn right in front of a cottage, and at a public footpath sign to Higher Poynton turn left over a stone stile, and follow a path across fields, heading downhill to rejoin the park boundary wall. Drop into a small wooded dell and out again, continue by the wall to a stile, climb over and keep ahead, above a steep wooded valley on the right, to a gate and stile. Climb that and continue down to a road (F).

Here turn right along a track in front of a small Methodist Church, cross a stream and turn right again through the West Park Gate (G) to re-enter Lyme Park. For the next ¾ mile (1 km), walk through a most attractive, steep-sided, wooded valley (ablaze with rhododendrons and azaleas in early summer) to a gate. Go through and bear right along the drive back to the hall and car park.

LE: 1:25 000 or 2½ INCHES to 1 MILE

9 Ashford in the Water and Monsal Dale

Start:	Ashford in the Water
Distance:	6 miles (9·5 km)
Approximate time:	3 hours
Parking:	Ashford in the Water
Refreshments:	Pubs and cafés in Ashford, pub and café at Monsal Head
Ordnance Survey maps:	Landranger 119 (Buxton, Matlock & Dovedale) and Outdoor Leisure 24 (The Peak District – White Peak area)

General description *A walk such as this, which combines one of the most idyllic villages and one of the finest viewpoints in the Peak District, superb woodland and some lovely stretches of riverside walking in Monsal Dale, is bound to be an intensely* pleasurable and memorable experience. Good clear footpaths, two gradual ascents and a modest distance add to the enjoyment and make it both an easy walk to accomplish and one worth taking plenty of time over.

Ashford in the Water is an exceptionally attractive village, its mainly eighteenth- and nineteenth-century limestone cottages situated amidst meadowland and clustered around the church, which was largely rebuilt in the late nineteenth century. The water of the title is the River Wye and the name of the village means exactly what it says – a ford near ash trees. The ford was an important link in an ancient routeway called the Old Portway, but was superseded in the seventeenth century by the construction of a three-arched pack-horse bridge, easily the most photographed structure in Ashford. This is known as the Sheepwash Bridge, because of the enclosure at one side of it, where sheep were held before being washed in the river prior to shearing. The church has two unusual features. One is the four virgin crants, decorated garlands which hang from

SCALE 1:25 000 or 2½ INCHES to 1 MILE

The superb view from Monsal Head

the roof and which used to be carried in the funeral processions of unmarried girls. The second is a table of Ashford black marble, a locally-quarried dark limestone which, when highly polished, took on a black appearance. Production of it only ceased in 1905.

From the car park behind the church, walk along Court Lane and turn right along Vicarage Lane. After about fifty yards (46 m), turn sharp left at a footpath sign for Monsal Dale, almost doubling back on your tracks, along a path that bears right, climbs some steps and continues up to a stile. Climb over and head across a field in a straight line, making for a stile in the top right-hand corner. Climb it and turn left along a winding, walled track (**A**) which gives glorious and expansive views over the surrounding countryside. Where the track ends, climb a stone stile and bear left along the edge of a field, climbing gently to another stone stile. Turn right at a footpath sign and keep ahead to join another walled track. Continue over several stiles to emerge at Monsal Head, and bear right to follow the head of the dale round to a road (**B**). Here is probably the finest of many fine views looking down the dale: the Wye winding gently and serenely below between meadows and the steep-sided wooded slopes of the dale, and the disused railway viaduct in the forefront of the scene, appearing to harmonise perfectly with its surroundings. This was not the view of Victorian conservationists who, led by Ruskin, bitterly opposed the desecration of the dale by the construction of what they felt was an ugly and intrusive structure. Time, the great healer, has weathered the viaduct which now appears to be part of, rather than an intrusion upon, the landscape. Perhaps in the late twenty-first century people will look back even on present-day concrete motorway bridges with some degree of affection. The viaduct was part of the Bakewell – Buxton section of the Midland Railway route from St Pancras to Manchester, which opened in 1863 and closed in 1968. Nowadays part of it forms the Monsal Trail, a footpath that almost links Buxton with Bakewell.

From the road take the path signposted to 'Monsal Dale, Viaduct and Trail', and drop down some steps. Keep straight ahead, ignoring the path to the left for 'Viaduct and Trail', and continue downhill between trees and shrubs. Turn left through a gate at the end of farm buildings, cross a footbridge over the River Wye, and turn left again (**C**). Now follows a delightful riverside walk of 1¼ miles (2 km). The path goes under the viaduct, past a weir, where the dale becomes narrower and more thickly wooded, and continues along the right-hand side of the winding river through a most beautiful wooded gorge to reach the main road (**D**).

Cross over, keep ahead across a car park drive and bear left along a path that heads up to a stile. Climb over and continue, following yellow arrows, to a marker post. Here bear left, following waymarks for Route 3, shortly afterwards turning left over a stone stile and heading uphill to another marker post. Turn left, ascending to a stile in a wall, climb that and continue ahead into Great Shacklow Wood.

The path keeps along the side of the valley through the steep-sided wood, gradually dropping down to join the river-bank by a former water mill that was used for crushing bones for fertiliser. Continue by the meandering Wye and over several stiles to reach a minor road (**E**). Turn left, right at the main road a few yards ahead and left over the picturesque Sheepwash Bridge back into Ashford village. Continue ahead along Fennel Street to the car park.

10 Tissington and Alsop en le Dale

Start:	Tissington
Distance:	6 miles (9·5 km)
Approximate time:	3 hours
Parking:	Tissington Trail car park just to the east of the village
Refreshments:	Café in Tissington
Ordnance Survey maps:	Landranger 119 (Buxton, Matlock & Dovedale) and Outdoor Leisure 24 (The Peak District – White Peak area)

General description The Peak District abounds in idyllic, unspoilt and un-commercialised villages of warm, honey-coloured limestone, and two of the finest of these feature in this walk. Also featured are two short stretches of the Tissington Trail, a former railway line now happily converted to a bridle-way and giving glorious sweeping views over the surrounding countryside. The walk involves a few modest climbs but nothing that could be described as strenuous.

Standing at the end of an avenue of limes, with cottages set back behind wide verges and church and hall facing each other across a spacious village street with a pond at one end of it, Tissington has an air of timeless serenity, and seems the quintessential English village. Part of the effect is undoubtedly due to the fact that Tissington is very much an estate village, which has been continuously in the possession of one family, the Fitzherberts, since the fifteenth century. The family still live in the fine early seventeenth-century hall, which has been extended and rebuilt several times over succeeding centuries. The simple church, overlooking both hall and village from its mound, still retains much Norman work, despite a thorough restoration in Victorian times, and possesses many monuments to the Fitz-herberts, as well as a rare Saxon font. Many of the cottages in the village date from a rebuilding programme carried out between 1830 and 1860, including the village school, now a tea-room, built in the year of Queen Victoria's accession (1837).

Although many villages in Derbyshire now hold annual Well Dressing ceremonies, Tissington is particularly associated with this ancient tradition, and various village wells are decorated with tableaux (usually depicting Biblical themes) made from pressing flowers, ferns, mosses, leaves and bark onto wooden frames covered with clay. The results are strikingly beautiful and ornate. Although the origins of this custom are somewhat obscure, the conventional theory is that it started during the Black Death, in the middle of the fourteenth century, as a thanksgiving for escaping the plague through the purity of the waters. It has not been a continuous custom, and it may have been first revived in Tissington as a result of its wells not running dry during a great drought in 1615. Whatever its origin, well-dressing is a colourful spectacle which attracts many visitors to Tissington on Ascension Day, and on various dates throughout the summer months to the other villages in the area which have taken up the custom.

From the Tissington Trail car park on the site of the former station, walk up to the lane and bear left into the village. In the village centre bear right, passing the church on the right and, a bit further on, Tissington Hall on the left, and keep ahead through the village to a junction **(A)**. Here ignore the tarmac lane that bears left and the broad track that bears right and instead climb a stone stile, at a public footpath sign to Alsop en le Dale, and take the field path straight ahead.

The path, though somewhat overgrown in summer, follows a fairly straight route, crossing two stone stiles in quick succession and then heading across a large field, making for a stone stile in a wall about 100 yards (92 m) to the right of a farm. Climb over, keep ahead to another stone stile, climb that and continue straight across the next field in the direction of farm buildings. At a metal gate bear right, by a fence on the left, to a stone stile at a wall corner. Climb over that, head downhill to another stone stile, climb that and keep ahead, past the farm buildings on the left, making for yet another stone stile in the top left-hand corner of the field. Climb over, turn right along a broad track, and just before a bridge ahead turn right through a gate, go up some steps and turn left to join the Tissington Trail **(B)**.

This was part of the railway line from Ashbourne to Buxton, opened in 1899 and finally closed in 1967. Fortunately the Peak Planning Board swiftly purchased large sections of it (as also other lines that closed around the same time) and converted it into a bridle-way that runs for thirteen miles between Parsley Hay and Ashbourne. The advantages for walkers, cyclists and riders are obvious: a flat, easy-to-follow, obstacle-free routeway, particularly suitable for the very young, elderly, disabled and unfit. Such converted lines can be monotonous if long distances are covered, but this walk utilises just two short stretches offering splendid views across the rolling countryside.

SCALE: 1:25 000 or 2½ INCHES to 1 MILE

Follow the trail for one mile (1·5 km) as far as a car park. Here turn right (C), at a public footpath sign for Alsop en le Dale, down to a stone stile, climb over and continue downhill along the edge of a field. About half-way down, look out for a gap in the wall on the right, go through, turn left and continue downhill along the edge of another field towards Alsop en le Dale, which is half-hidden by trees in the valley below. Climb a stone stile and turn right along the lane into the village – another peaceful and attractive one, smaller and less frequented than Tissington but with a similar combination of tiny picturesque Norman church, old hall opposite it and houses, farms and cottages.

The next part of the route seems somewhat complex after the simplicity of the Tissington Trail involving climbing over lots of stiles. Walk through the village and, just past the last house on the left, turn left up a bank (D), go over a stile and turn right over a stone stile. Bear slightly left and continue across a field, making for another stone stile. Climb that and bear slightly left again, heading uphill to a stone stile in the wall in front. After climbing that, turn right, keeping parallel with the wall, and heading towards a group of trees. Climb another stone stile, walk through the middle of a small wood, go over a stile at the far end and continue by a wall on the right. Climb another stone stile and keep ahead, dropping down towards the valley in front, climbing yet another stone stile and continuing in a straight line over several more. Go straight across a tarmac drive and keep ahead, bearing slightly right to the bottom right-hand edge of a field. Here climb a partially-hidden stone stile and continue to a road.

Turn left along the road for nearly ½ mile (0·8 km) and, just after passing a barn and opposite a public footpath sign on the left, turn right (E) into a field and follow the edge of it (no clear path) uphill to a meeting of paths. Turn right along a path lined with trees to a stile, climb over, turn left along the edge of a field and climb another stile to start heading downhill. Bear slightly right over a ditch and then turn left, continuing down to the bottom of the valley, over a footbridge and straight up the middle of the field ahead. Go through a gap in a wall, keep ahead (still climbing), bear right through some trees and then left. Where the path emerges from the trees, bear half-right and head across a field to a stone stile by a gate.

Climb over, turn left by a bridge and climb another stile to rejoin the Tissington Trail (F). Keep along it for 1½ miles (2·25 km), with more fine views all the way, back to the car park.

35

11 Castleton and Mam Tor

Start:	Castleton
Distance:	6 miles (9·5 km)
Approximate time:	3 hours
Parking:	Castleton
Refreshments:	Plenty of pubs and cafés in Castleton
Ordnance Survey maps:	Landranger 110 (Sheffield & Huddersfield) and Outdoor Leisure 1 (The Peak District – Dark Peak area)

General description *Castleton occupies an enviable position near the head of the Hope valley, dominated by the ruins of Peveril Castle and surrounded by steep hills and rolling moors. The walk begins with a long, steady ascent of Cave Dale, flattens out for a while and then continues with a shorter but steeper climb to the 1,695 ft (508 m) summit of Mam Tor. After that comes one of the finest scenic ridge walks in the Peak District, with the Vale of Edale on one side and the Hope valley on the other, before the route drops down to return to Castleton. Leave plenty of time at the end to visit some of the caves near the village perhaps, and (despite the daunting-looking climb) explore the castle ruins.*

0	200	400	600	800 m	1		Kilometres	

SCALE 1:25 000 or 2½ INCHES to 1 MILE

0	200	400	600	800	1000 yds		Miles 1

Cave Dale overlooked by the dramatic ruins of Peveril Castle

With such a multitude of man-made and natural attractions nearby, it is no wonder that Castleton has become one of the principal tourist centres of the Peak District. It grew up around the base of Peveril Castle, which was founded in the late eleventh century by William Peverel, an illegitimate son of William the Conqueror. The castle occupies a virtually impregnable position, with steep cliffs on three sides; it seems likely that initially a curtain wall was constructed only on the north side facing the town, and that the other three sides relied on the natural defence afforded by those cliffs. Its most outstanding feature is the great keep, built by Henry II in 1176, by which time the castle had been forfeited to the Crown. As well as being a defensive stronghold, it also served as a hunting lodge for the Royal Forest of the Peak, before falling into disuse and subsequent ruin in the fifteenth century.

In the village itself the major building is the church which, though mainly a nineteenth-century restoration, retains its fine Norman chancel arch. However, the feature which most draws visitors to Castleton is the varied and spectacular caverns in its vicinity, a mixture of natural caves and caverns created as a result of mining for lead and other minerals. Prominent among them are the Peak, Blue John, Treak Cliff and Speedwell Caverns, the latter being particularly exciting to visit as it involves a subterranean boat trip.

Turn left out of the car park and turn right by the church up through the Market Place. At the top turn left and, a few yards ahead, turn right into a narrow entrance between cottages by a footpath sign for Cave Dale **(A)**. Climb a stile and follow an uphill path through the narrow dale, at first through an almost perpendicular gorge below the towering cliffs on the right that are crowned by Peveril Castle. The rocky path climbs towards the head of the dale and continues, by a wall on the right, to a metal gate. Go through and keep ahead, following yellow waymarks to another gate. Pass through that and continue across a large field, heading down to a sheep pen and climbing a stile to reach a path junction **(B)**.

Climb another stile and turn right along a broad, walled track across wild and open country, dotted with the remains of abandoned lead mines. Where this walled track ends, keep ahead by a wall on the left along the edges of two fields, up to a footpath sign in front of a gate and stile **(C)**. Here turn right and, keeping along the edge of a wall on the left, climb two stiles and head downhill, bearing gently to the left in the direction of the distinctive bulk of Mam Tor. Mam Tor is known as the 'Shivering Mountain' on account of the instability of its lower layers of loose, soft shales, which are constantly crumbling and falling, giving the impression that the hill is moving or shivering. It is this instability that led to the closure of the A625 (Sheffield to Chapel-en-le-Frith road) some years ago, causing traffic to be diverted up Winnat's Pass, a narrow route between steep limestone cliffs.

The path leads down to the road **(D)** near the top of Winnat's Pass where you cross over, bearing a few yards to the right to a gate and stile. Pass through and keep by a wall on the left, crossing Windy Knoll, to a stile. Climb over, cross a road, climb another stile opposite and continue along a grassy uphill path to yet another stile. Climb that, go up some steps, turn right over a stile **(E)** and continue up a stepped path for the final stage, steep but made easy by the steps, to the top of Mam Tor. From the top the views are magnificent: to the left is the vale of Edale with the Pennine Way clearly seen snaking its way up towards Kinder Scout; to the right the superb view over Castleton, Peveril Castle and the Hope valley is marred only by the Hope Cement Works; behind stretches the ridge path along Rushup Edge, and in front is the exhilarating ridge walk now to be followed to Hollins Cross. This gives the most outstanding views, on both sides and ahead, over a typical English landscape at its best – on the lower slopes a lovely patchwork of green fields, criss-crossed by hedges and dotted with trees, villages and farmsteads, and, behind, the bare moorlands crossed by stone walls.

After a while you drop down to Hollins Cross, a crossroads of paths. The ridge path continues ahead climbing up to Lose Hill. The alternative name for this hill is Ward's Piece, after a Sheffield man, G.H.B. Ward, who made a major contribution to the cause of rambling in the local area. But here the route turns right **(F)**, heading steeply downhill in the direction of Castleton, which is clearly visible ahead, to join a farm track. Follow the track back to the village, with impressive views of Peveril Castle in front all the time.

On reaching Castleton keep ahead at the main road, bearing right, back to the car park.

12 Cromford and Matlock Bath

Start:	Cromford
Distance:	6 miles (9·5 km), or two separate walks of 3 miles (4·75 km) each
Approximate time:	3 hours, or 1½ hours for each of the two separate walks
Parking:	Cromford
Refreshments:	Pubs and cafés at Cromford, pub at Starkholmes, pubs and cafés at Matlock Bath
Ordnance Survey maps:	Landranger 119 (Buxton, Matlock & Dovedale) and Outdoor Leisure 24 (The Peak District – White Peak area)

General description *A quite incredible variety of scenic and historic attractions are packed into this modestly-distanced and thoroughly absorbing walk. The scenic wonders comprise the Black Rocks of Cromford, both impressive in themselves and an excellent vantage point, and the narrow gorge of the Derwent. The historic features are a Victorian spa and the fascinating village of Cromford, one of the cradles of the Industrial Revolution. As this is a figure-of-eight route around Cromford, it can easily be converted into two separate, shorter walks.*

In 1771 Sir Richard Arkwright, a Lancashire cotton entrepreneur, established the first successful water-powered cotton mill in the then scattered and tiny farming community of Cromford, an event which led to the transformation of textile manufacturing from a cottage-based into a factory-based industry. The main advantage of Cromford was the water power from the River Derwent, but it did have two disadvantages: poor communications and a shortage of labour. The shortage of labour was solved by building a new community to attract workers, and ultimately the problem of poor communications was solved by the construction of first a canal and later a railway and main road through the area. But Cromford was still a long way from the main centres of the cotton industry, and therefore never developed into another Manchester or Bolton. What is left today is a rare example of an early Industrial Revolution textile settlement, which has retained many of the original buildings erected by Arkwright and his successors.

Some of these structures are seen near the start of the walk, which begins opposite Arkwright's Mill, a complex of buildings, from the late eighteenth century onwards, now being painstakingly excavated and restored by the Arkwright Society. Turn right along the road, soon passing the Cromford Canal Wharf on the right. The canal was opened in 1793, closed in 1944 and has now been restored for pleasure trips. Next comes the church, built towards the end of the eighteenth century and enlarged and altered in the middle of the nineteenth. It was originally a private chapel for the Arkwrights, and Sir Richard is buried in it. Shortly afterwards turn left over the Derwent and ahead is the entrance to Willersley Castle, also built for Sir Richard Arkwright in the late eighteenth century and now used as a Methodist guest house.

Turn right and immediately left up a lane signposted to Starkholmes **(A)**, and follow it for one mile (1·5 km), at first steeply uphill (later it flattens out). From the lane there are magnificent views to the left over Matlock Bath and the Derwent Gorge. Opposite the White Lion Inn at Starkholmes turn sharp left **(B)**, at a public footpath sign to Matlock Bath, along a winding downhill path. Turn left at a T-junction of paths and continue down by the edge of trees, past the cable car station and under the railway bridge, into Matlock Bath. Turn left along the riverside path and right over the bridge by the station car park **(C)**.

Matlock Bath, an extension of Matlock itself, became a popular spa resort in the nineteenth century, especially after the construction of the main road and railway through the Derwent Gorge. Victorian visitors came mainly to take the waters and enjoy the scenery; attractions to delight twentieth-century tourists are the riverside gardens, splendid autumn illuminations, visits to caves and old lead mines and a wide range of pubs, restaurants and cafés. The latest amenities are the Peak District Mining Museum, housed in the former Pavilion, and the cable cars which provide a spectacular crossing of the gorge and take visitors up to the Heights of Abraham where, in fine weather, superb Swiss-looking views can be enjoyed from the terrace of an imitation Swiss chalet. It is not only the twentieth century which has appreciated the similarities with Switzerland – in the nineteenth century Joseph Paxton built the railway station also in the style of a Swiss chalet.

Turn left along the main road through the town and, opposite the Peak District Mining Museum **(D)**, bear right past the Fishpond Hotel up to the higher road. Turn right and almost immediately left, looking out for steps ahead. Now comes a climb up a very steep, stepped path which zigzags through dense woodland, and upon reaching the top turn left along a narrow lane through the secluded hamlet of Upperwood. Keep ahead at a 'No Through Road' sign, along what is now a track, past houses, continuing along a narrow woodland path at a public footpath sign to Scarthin. The walk through this steep-sided wood is very pleasant and occasional gaps on the left reveal fine views over the valley, including the Victorian fantasy of Riber Castle on the skyline and later a brief glimpse of Masson Mill, which includes part of the original building erected by Sir Richard Arkwright in 1783–84. Start to descend, turning left on meeting another path and finally dropping down a cobbled path to a lane opposite the Primitive Methodist Chapel in Scarthin, a former lead-mining settlement.

Turn right down to the main road and turn sharp left at the road, past the corn mill and pond, into the village centre of Cromford (**E**). (*This is the point at which the walk can be shortened.*) Turn right uphill, making a brief detour on the left to admire the rows of three-storeyed houses in North Street, built by Arkwright in 1776–77, the earliest planned industrial housing in Britain and greatly in advance of its time. Shortly afterwards turn left along Bedehouse Lane, soon bearing right along a tarmac path that climbs up between walls, with striking views of the Black Rocks ahead on the skyline. The path winds between the gardens of the houses and cottages, crosses a road and keeps ahead at a public footpath sign up to a T-junction. Here turn left along a track, soon bearing right and continuing uphill, turning left at a sign for the Black Rocks and High Peak Trail. Pass through two gates, keep ahead through woodland and climb a stone stile, turning right along the High Peak Trail (**F**). This was part of the old Cromford and High Peak Railway, converted into a public bridle-way after the line closed in 1967. Follow the pleasantly wooded and shady track as far as the Black Rocks, making a short detour to the left to explore this impressive collection of massive gritstone boulders, from where there is a magnificent panoramic view over Cromford, Matlock, Riber Castle, High Tor and the Heights of Abraham (**G**).

Retrace your steps to where the High Peak Trail was first joined (**F**). Here turn left over a stone stile, immediately turn right over another stile and walk along a grassy downhill path from which all the main sights of Cromford can be seen below in one glance – the village itself, the church, Willersley Castle and Masson Mill. Go through a gap in a wall, bear right along the side of the hill to a stone stile, climb over and keep ahead into woodland. Approaching a

Arkwright's Cromford — a cradle of the Industrial Revolution

wall on the left, turn sharp left onto a lower path (**H**) and continue along that path, by a wall on the right. Soon the path becomes a road, continuing downhill past houses to a main road. Cross over, go through a gap in a wall opposite and follow a narrow path for the short distance back to the car park opposite Arkwright's Mill.

SCALE: 1:25 000 or 2½ INCHES to 1 MILE

13 The Goyt valley and Shining Tor

Start:	Errwood Reservoir
Distance:	6½ miles (10·25 km)
Approximate time:	3½ hours
Parking:	Car park near end of Errwood Reservoir. On Bank Holidays and summer Sundays, when there is no access by car, park instead at Pym Chair **(B)** and start and finish the walk there
Refreshments:	None
Ordnance Survey maps:	Landranger 118 (Stoke-on-Trent & Macclesfield) and 119 (Buxton, Matlock & Dovedale), Outdoor Leisure 24 (The Peak District – White Peak area)

General description *The character of the Goyt valley has been somewhat altered over the last half century. Its former isolation has been virtually ended by the growing influx of car-borne visitors (indeed, a vehicle restriction scheme operates on Sundays and Bank Holidays during the summer months), and its natural beauty has been modified by the planting of conifers and the construction of reservoirs. Although to some extent, therefore, more artificial than natural, the valley's beauty is still outstanding, with its combination of moorland, woodland, streams and fine views, while the reservoirs and plantations, now softened and made more natural-looking by the passage of time, can both be said to add an extra dimension to its attractiveness. This walk encompasses some of the most interesting features and grandest scenery here, climbing by the scanty ruins of an abandoned hall and most unusual shrine to the Shining Tor ridge, and continuing along the ridge with splendid views on both sides to the summit of Shining Tor, before dropping back into the wooded valley.*

The Goyt valley was formerly a remote area of wild and open country lying between two royal hunting grounds, Peak Forest to the east and Macclesfield Forest to the west. It was partially 'tamed' in the nineteenth century, both by the activities of the Grimshawe family, who built Errwood Hall and laid out the surrounding ornamental gardens, and by the growth of industry in the area, notably quarrying and some coal-mining. More major and significant changes to its landscape came in the present century, with the damming of the river by Stockport Corporation to create two reservoirs, Fernilee in 1938 and Errwood in 1967, and the planting by the Forestry Commission of large blocks of conifers, mainly on the western slopes, beginning in 1963.

With your back to the reservoir, follow the direction of a Woodland Walk sign uphill across grass and through a gap in a wall, to enter the former grounds of Errwood Hall. Continue through a most attractive, steep, thickly-wooded valley and turn sharp right at another Woodland Walk sign, passing the remains of the hall on the left. Errwood Hall was built by the Grimshawes, a Roman Catholic family who owned much of the valley, in 1830, and photographs of it indicate that it was a most handsome and palatial Italian-looking residence, surrounded by exotic landscaped gardens. It was abandoned and demolished in the 1930s, when the waters of the first of the reservoirs started to rise, but the ruins, meagre though they are, have an attractively melancholic air, and some vestiges of the ornamental gardens still remain, especially the vast number of rhododendrons and azaleas, resplendent in late May and June.

Keep ahead, by the stream on the right, dropping down to cross the stream by stepping-stones and continuing along the side of the valley, below Foxlow Edge on the right, climbing up towards a road. On the left is an excellent view of the ridge soon to be traversed, and just before you reach the road the Spanish Shrine is passed on the left. This small, simple, circular building, utterly incongruous in such a setting, is English in construction (built of solid local gritstone) but undeniably Mediterranean in design and inspiration. It was erected by the Grimshawes in 1889 in memory of a much-loved Spanish governess in their employ.

Continue to the road **(A)** and turn left up to the top of the ridge at Pym Chair, a superb viewpoint looking to the right over the Goyt woodlands and hills beyond, and a crossroads of ancient routeways, including a 'saltway' from the Cheshire salt-producing district around Northwich and Nantwich across to Chesterfield and Sheffield. Just below a car park turn left **(B)** up some steps to a public footpath sign to Shining Tor. Now begins a grand ridge walk of nearly 2 miles (3 km), first over Cats Tor (1,703 ft (511 m)) and then on to Shining Tor (1,833 ft (550 m)), keeping by a broken wall on the right all the way. The views over the rolling hills and bare moorlands on both sides are superb, especially that towards the distinctive, conical-shaped Shutlingsloe from the trig. point marking the summit of Shining Tor, which is reached by a few yards' detour to the right over a ladder stile **(C)**.

Turn left by the summit, still keeping by a wall on the right, and head first downhill and then up again to a ladder stile. Climb over and continue ahead a few yards to a junction of paths. Here turn right, keep ahead to another ladder stile, climb that and, about 50 yards (46 m) ahead, turn left through a gap in a wall at a footpath sign to Goytsclough **(D)**. The path heads downhill (with striking views of the moorlands ahead on the other side of the valley), by the side of conifer plantations,

which you enter after climbing a ladder stile. Continue ahead, cross a stream and later bear left along a grassy path, climbing a stile at the edge of the woods and finally turning sharp left **(E)** down to a road.

Turn left along the road. This leads directly back to the starting point, but fortunately there are much pleasanter alternatives to a 1 mile (1·5 km) walk on tarmac. At the first group of trees turn right **(F)**, dropping steeply to the bottom of the valley, and turn left along a very attractive wooded path that keeps mostly along a ledge just above the River Goyt. Where the path rejoins the road, cross straight over onto an opposite path (public footpath sign to Errwood Hall), which keeps parallel with the road and gives fine views over Errwood Reservoir ahead. After about ½ mile (0·8 km), turn right across open grassland down to the car park.

SCALE: 1:25 000 or 2½ INCHES to 1 MILE

14 The Manifold valley

Start:	Wetton
Distance:	7 miles (11·25 km)
Approximate time:	4 hours
Parking:	Wetton
Refreshments:	Pub at Wetton, café at Wetton Mill
Ordnance Survey maps:	Landranger 119 (Buxton, Matlock & Dovedale) and Outdoor Leisure 24 (The Peak District – White Peak area)

SCALE: 1:25 000 or 2½ INCHES to 1 MILE

General description The Manifold flows roughly parallel with the Dove, through similarly attractive limestone scenery, but its valley is generally quieter and less well known. The name Manifold means literally many folds or turns, and is an apt one, for the river forms a whole series of loops and meanders along its length. From the village of Wetton the walk proceeds in an undulating manner across fields, passing the remains of abandoned copper mines and eventually climbing to a most dramatic and expansive viewpoint overlooking the Manifold valley. A steep descent into the valley is followed by a lovely walk along the Manifold Track, a disused railway line that keeps by the winding river. The return to Wetton is via a detour to the impressive Thor's Cave, without doubt the dominant feature of the surrounding landscape.

The small, remote and seemingly unchanging village of Wetton lies on the eastern slopes of the Manifold valley, its attractive grey stone cottages grouped around the pub and medieval church, a short and plain building with a rather heavy-looking tower. From the car park turn left along a lane and left again at a road junction, walking through the village and passing both pub and church. Where the road bends left, keep ahead along a tarmac track at a public footpath sign to 'Back of Ecton' (A). Go through a gate, continue to to a stone stile, climb over and keep ahead to another stone stile at a National Trust sign to Wetton Hill. Climb that and proceed across the middle of a field between hills on both sides, the smooth flanks of Wetton Hill being on the left. Head down to a stile in a wire fence, climb over and continue across a field towards a wall, bearing right to another stile.

Climb over and, with a lovely view in front of you of rolling hills punctuated by random groups of trees, first keep ahead by a wall on the left. At the end of the wall bear slightly left along a grassy path (just about discernible), making for the far left-hand corner of a long field. Here climb a stile, continue to another stile, climb that, cross a walled track and climb another stile directly opposite, heading up to a higher track. Turn right, and where the track forks keep ahead, climbing gently (B). Just before the brow of the hill, turn right through a metal gate and along a grassy path that heads towards a wall. Keeping by that wall on the left, walk past the workings of abandoned copper mines on the right, to a stile. Climb over and continue along what is now a ridge path, with grand views on both sides, still keeping by the wall on the left. On entering a large field with the remains of several mine workings, bear slightly right and head across to the trig. point marking the summit of Ecton Hill. A few yards in front is the top of an escarpment from which there is a magnificent view over the Manifold valley, with the village of Warslow on the horizon, and, below, Dale Bridge and a prominent house which looks as if it belongs more to the Rhineland than to Staffordshire.

Turn right along a grassy path, go through a gap in a broken wall and ahead to a stile in a wall on the left. Climb over, and head downhill along the edge of a field by a wire fence on the right, following the field boundary sharply to the left and dropping more steeply through trees to a stile. Climb over, turn right under an arch, pass the house which looks like a Rhenish castle and go down a track to a road. Continue ahead towards Dale Bridge, and just before it turn left through a gate onto the Manifold Track (C).

This is a footpath created in 1937 by Staffordshire County Council from the disused Leek and Manifold Light Railway, a single-track line which carried mainly milk and a few tourists and was only in existence between 1904 and 1934. The only criticism I have, a slight one, is that the path was tarmacked, unlike more recent conversions of ex-railway tracks into footpaths and bridle-ways; this gives it a somewhat artificial look, but it is easy and pleasant to walk along.

Follow the track by the winding Manifold (easy to see here how the river acquired its name), through the wooded steep-sided valley for ¾ mile (1 km) to a lane, and keep ahead under a tunnel (D). Between here and just below Wetton Mill the track becomes a public road but few vehicles use it – it is still mainly frequented by walkers and cyclists. Continue for 1¼ miles (2 km) to Wetton Mill, which lies to the left just over an old pack-horse bridge. The attractive building was a corn mill, which closed in 1857, and is now a farm and conveniently situated café. The pack-horse bridge was used for carrying copper from the mines on Ecton Hill which were passed earlier in the walk, and which were at one time among the most productive copper mines in Europe.

Below Wetton Mill there is a choice of two parallel routes below the sheer limestone cliffs on the left – a particularly attractive section of the Manifold valley. Cross a bridge, continue to where the two routes rejoin and keep ahead to recross the river. At this point the Manifold Track reverts to being just a footpath. Soon Thor's Cave can be seen ahead and it is here that the Manifold disappears through swallow or shake holes to flow underground (hence the often dry river-bed), reappearing near Ilam Hall.

Just below the cave turn left over a footbridge to cross the river again (E), keep ahead through a narrow gap in a fence and continue up through dense woodland, turning sharp right at a footpath sign to make a detour, through the woods and up steps to Thor's Cave. From this great yawning gap, from which evidence of prehistoric occupation has been unearthed, there is a magnificent view looking up the valley.

Retrace your steps, turning right to rejoin the path to Wetton, and continue through trees to a stile. Climb over and head across a field – perhaps looking back to admire the superb view of Thor's Cave, the wooded valley and the spire of Butterton Church on the skyline – up to a stone stile by a yellow marker post. Climb over and continue towards the houses of Wetton, turning left over a stone stile just before a gate at the far end of the field. Turn right along a lane, right again at a junction, and on reaching a T-junction turn left to the car park.

15 Hathersage

Start:	Hathersage
Distance:	7 miles (11·25 km). Shorter version 3½ miles (5·5 km)
Approximate time:	3½ hours (2 hours for shorter version)
Parking:	Hathersage
Refreshments:	Pubs and cafés at Hathersage
Ordnance Survey maps:	Landranger 110 (Sheffield & Huddersfield) and Pathfinder 743 (Sheffield)

General description *The Derwent valley around Hathersage is a mixture of delightful meadows, wooded valleys and rolling hills, backed by open moorland and, beyond, by gritstone outcrops which form some of the famous gritstone edges. The walk explores some of this glorious hilly countryside, on both the north and south sides of the river, and the views over the valley, from all angles, are magnificent throughout. Near the end of the walk the grave of a well known, semi-mythical figure is passed.*

Hathersage, recently enlarged as a result of its popularity as a commuter area for Sheffield, is a most attractive jumble of old cottages and farmhouses, former needle mills, modern housing estates, wine bars, inns and tea-shops. It occupies a fine position above the River Derwent, surrounded by outstandingly beautiful scenery, which makes it difficult to envisage it as a dirty and smoky industrial village, as it was in the nineteenth century. Then it was a centre for the manufacture of pins and needles – a particularly unhealthy industry because of the dust caused by the grinding of the points on the pins and needles.

Two well known people, one real and one semi-mythical, have close connections with Hathersage. One is Little John, right-hand man of Robin Hood, and whose alleged grave (passed near the end of the walk) is in the churchyard. The other is Charlotte Brontë, who stayed at Hathersage and used the name of the local lords of the manor, the Eyres, for the heroine of her best-known book. The fine fourteenth-century church with its spire stands high above the village and contains the tombs of many members of the Eyre family, for whose excellent brasses it is noted.

Turn right out of the car park, opposite the swimming baths, and then first left. Turn right down Dore Lane, go under a railway bridge, and just before the gate and lodge of Nether Hall in front, turn left **(A)** over a stone stile and walk along the edge of fields to the main road. Here turn right over Leadmill Bridge and right again, through a gap and over a stile **(B)**, to follow a path by the Derwent.

Just past a weir, bear left away from the riverside path, climb a stile, head across to another stile, climb that and continue up the slope ahead to yet another stone stile at the top. Climb that and turn right along the edge of a field, by a line of trees and a wall on the right, climb a stile by a gate and continue towards a farm. Having gained some height, you now get lovely views across the valley to Hathersage and the wooded hills and high moors beyond. Climb another stile, turn right down a track towards Broadhay Farm, cross a beck (with the somewhat unromantic name of Dunge Brook) and immediately turn left through a gate, at a public footpath sign, and head across a field, keeping along a ledge just above the beck.

Climb a stile to enter Dunge Wood and keep ahead through the wood, joining a wall on the right and turning right through a gate in that wall. Continue uphill across a field, passing the right-hand side of a farm, to a gate. Go through, bear left along a track, and after passing a cattle grid turn sharp right along an uphill tarmac lane. The lane levels off, giving more excellent views, this time including the village of Hope and Win Hill, and drops down to Offerton, bending right to pass Offerton Hall, one of seven large farmhouses in the area said to have been provided by Robert and Elizabeth Eyre for their seven sons, in the fourteenth century. Just past the hall, bear right through a gate **(C)** and head diagonally downhill to a stone stile. Climb over and continue down, over another stile, to a signpost. Keep ahead for a few yards to cross some stepping-stones over the Derwent. (After rain this is sometimes impossible; in that case an easy alternative is to turn right and follow the riverside path back to Leadmill Bridge.) Continue up some steps, go over a stile and bear left, heading straight across fields to a road. Turn right along the road.

At this point, those wishing only to do the shorter version of the walk can continue straight along the road back to the centre of Hathersage.

For the longer version, turn first left along Hill Foot and over a railway bridge. Shortly afterwards turn left up steps **(D)** between houses and continue uphill along a narrow stony path, between a fence and a hedge. Where this path ends, climb a stile and continue along a grassy path, over a series of stiles and gates, to a lane. Turn left along the lane, bear left at a junction, and shortly afterwards turn left through a gate, at a public bridle-way sign to Hurstclough and Bamford. Keep ahead by a line of trees to a gate, go through, bear left downhill and turn right, by a hedge on the left, continuing down towards trees ahead. Cross a brook,

bear left up to a stile, climb over and keep ahead along a track at a public bridle-way sign. Continue through a metal gate and along a sunken path between hedges to another metal gate.

Go through and turn right along a green lane lined with hedges, called Hurstclough Lane (E). Keep along it for nearly ½ mile

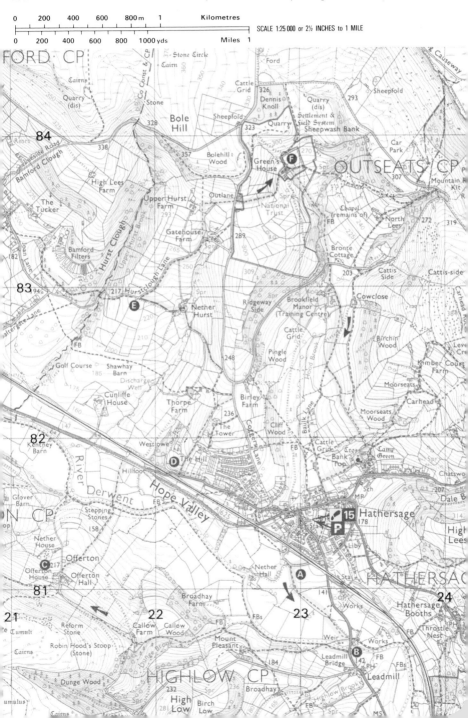

Hathersage Church – high up above the village and the Derwent valley

(0·8 km) until the point where it turns slightly to the right. Here look out for a stile in the hedge on the left (not easy to see but by the side of a large tree), climb over, turn right along the edge of a field, climb a stile, continue ahead to another stile, climb that and bear right to a gate. Pass through and bear right across the next field, making for a gate in a wall near a wire fence at the far end.

Go through, cross a lane and continue along a drive that is just slightly to the right. Walk past a house, climb a stile by a cattle grid and keep ahead along a straight path, with a dramatic view of the valley ahead and Stanage Edge standing out prominently on the skyline. The path curves left to a large farm (Greens House) and passes behind the farm. Go through a gate and immediately turn right over a stone stile (**F**). Keep along the edge of a field to descend the lovely valley of Hood Brook, cradled by wooded hills. Pass through a gate and keep ahead through several more gates, across fields and through delightful woodland by Hood Brook, down to a lane. The ruined chapel, visible on the hillside to the left before you enter the woods, belonged to North Lees, a large farmhouse and another of the seven Eyre halls around Hathersage.

Cross the lane, go through a gate opposite (public footpath sign to Hathersage) and head across a field, bearing left by the wall of Brookfield Manor (another likely Eyre residence) and keeping ahead to a stile. Climb over and continue to a signpost, bearing slightly right and joining a track up to another stile. Climb that, keep ahead to the next stile, climb over and turn left along the edge of a field, by a hedge and fence on the left. At this stage there are more outstanding views over the Derwent and Hope valleys. Keep along the edge of the field to a stile, climb over and continue, by a hedge and later a wire fence on the right, dropping down to a footbridge over a brook. Climb a stile and head uphill, bearing right at the top and going over another stile to a lane. Keep ahead to enter Hathersage churchyard.

The church is well worth visiting in its own right but most visitors come here to view the grave of Little John in the churchyard. Whether Little John, or indeed any of the Sherwood outlaws, ever really existed is debatable, but when this grave was opened in 1784, a thigh-bone 32 in. long was found in it, indicating a man about 7 ft tall. Little John's supposed grave is just one of many connections between this area and Robin Hood. A large stone near Offerton is called Robin Hood's Stoop, a cave on Stanage Edge is known as Robin Hood's Cave, there may be a connection in the name of Hood Brook, and many of the legends claim that Robin Hood was born at Loxley, which is only a few miles away.

Turn right in front of the south porch of the church and continue through the churchyard, through a gate and along a path ahead, then through a succession of gates, down to a lane. Turn left into the village centre, cross over the main street and take the path opposite, which leads directly back to the car park.

16 A Five Dales Walk

Start:	Tideswell
Distance:	7½ miles (12 km)
Approximate time:	4 hours
Parking:	Tideswell
Refreshments:	Pubs and cafés in Tideswell, pub in Litton
Ordnance Survey maps:	Landranger 119 (Buxton, Matlock & Dovedale) and Outdoor Leisure 24 (The Peak District – White Peak area)

General description *The five dales which are featured in this walk are, in order,*

Tansley, Cressbrook, Water-cum-Jolly, Miller's and Tideswell, and each one is distinctive and attractive. Evidence of former industrial activity can be seen along the banks of the Wye at Cressbrook and Litton Mills, and the walk begins at a fine church known as the 'Cathedral of the Peak'. In a walk based predominantly in the dales, the going is inevitably easy and fairly flat, apart from some climbing along both sides of Cressbrook Dale. The section along the banks of the Wye through the adjacent Water-cum-Jolly and Miller's Dales is outstandingly beautiful.

Tideswell is one of those places that is difficult to categorise – is it a large village or small town? It is the size of a village but has the bustle and appearance of a busy market town, and its large and imposing church,

justifiably nicknamed the 'Cathedral of the Peak', would put many a parish church in much larger towns to shame. It is a predominantly fourteenth-century building with a fine porch, a tall, pinnacled west tower and, unusually for a village church, two transepts. Inside, it is spacious and dignified with some old tombs and ornate nineteenth-century wood carving. In the later Middle Ages, Tideswell became an important market town and lead-mining centre, and the church was built during its heyday. The town later declined and faded into relative obscurity, which is why it is now overshadowed by its splendid church.

From the parking area in Cherry Tree Square turn left, and at the memorial monument bear right along a back lane. Just before the Post Office, turn right at a public footpath sign, along a path which climbs up above the village by a series of steps, giving a fine view over both church and village. Keep ahead at the top to a lane, turn right and follow the lane for ¾ mile (1 km) into the village of Litton, a small but spacious village of fine seventeenth- and eighteenth-century houses, grouped around a triangular green and lining the wide main street which leads from it.

Walk past the small modern church, and in the village centre bear left along the main street. At a public footpath sign to Wardlow, turn right (A) and immediately left, climbing a stone stile at the side of a house. Head diagonally across a field to the bottom left-hand corner, climb another stone stile, bear left for a few yards along a walled track, and at the next public footpath sign turn right and walk across the middle of a narrow field to another footpath sign. All around is a most pleasant and attractive landscape of small fields criss-crossed by stone walls – typical of this part of the Peak District. At the public footpath sign bear left, head downhill to a wall corner, climb a stile and continue down to the foot of the shallow dry valley. This is Tansley Dale, a short and narrow tributary dale, and you keep along the path through it to a stile at the bottom.

Climb over and turn right to join Cressbrook Dale, a beautiful, quiet, smooth, steep-sided valley. After a few hundred yards the valley curves to the right but the path keeps ahead, climbing steeply from the valley bottom towards a wall and stone stile. Before reaching the wall, turn right (B) and follow the top edge of the dale, making for the corner of another wall. At this point there are superb views to the right, with the cottages and farms of Litton still visible on the horizon. A little further on, the sides of the dale become thickly wooded and steeper, and the path starts dropping down to the valley bottom, where it crosses a footbridge. Continue straight ahead on the other side, climbing again and keeping by the edge of the trees on the right. There are more good views from this path, this time over to the left, where there are almost perpendicular cliffs on the other side of the dale. The path continues through woodland to join a tarmac road which you follow down to Cressbrook, where the dale enters the main valley of the River Wye.

At the bottom of the hill turn right (C), at a footpath sign for Monsal Dale, Monsal Trail and Litton Mill, passing behind the handsome, but at present semi-derelict, Cressbrook Mill, built in 1815. Bear right, walk through a quarry, cross a footbridge and keep ahead, below overhanging cliffs along the banks of the Wye, through Water-cum-Jolly Dale, the rather odd name given to a short section of the dale just to the west of Cressbrook Mill. At this stage the dale is sheer, almost perpendicular, and thickly wooded at its lower levels, but above are smooth-sided grassy hillsides, dotted with limestone outcrops. The river-bed here is choked with trees, bushes, reeds and marshy grass.

The river later becomes wider and clearer and enters the delightful Miller's Dale. The whole of this section by the Wye, nearly 1½ miles (2·25 km), is as glorious a stretch of riverside walking as can be found anywhere in the Peak District. Walk through the Litton Mill complex of buildings and continue along a tarmac lane, passing a row of houses on the right, and keeping by the river all the while.

At a public footpath sign to Tideswell Dale, bear right off the tarmac lane (D) along a wooded path below cliffs on the right. The path winds through Tideswell Dale, the fifth and last dale, first on the left-hand side of a narrow stream and later crossing a footbridge and keeping along the other bank, curving right to a car park and picnic area. Walk through the car park and along a path ahead, which is lined with an impressive row of trees, to a road.

Keep along this road for ¼ mile (0·4 km) (there is a path on the left-hand side). Just past the end of a small sewage works on the left, and about fifty yards (46 m) before the road starts to curve to the left, look out for a stile on the left (not easy to see) (E). Climb it and take the path ahead, which climbs for a few yards and then turns right along the side of the dale, gradually ascending between trees and shrubs to join a farm track. Turn right along this track and follow it, by a wall on the left, back to Tideswell. On reaching a lane, turn right down to the road, and left into the village centre.

17 Three Shire Heads and Axe Edge Moor

Start:	Cat and Fiddle Inn
Distance:	7½ miles (12 km)
Approximate time:	4 hours
Parking:	Small parking area opposite Cat and Fiddle
Refreshments:	Cat and Fiddle Inn
Ordnance Survey maps:	Landranger 118 (Stoke-on-Trent & Macclesfield) and 119 (Buxton, Matlock & Dovedale), Outdoor Leisure 24 (The Peak District – White Peak area)

General description *There could be no greater contrast than between this walk, mostly over open moorland, and those in the softer, gentler scenery of the limestone dales. It begins nearly 1,700 ft (510 m) up at a well known inn on the Macclesfield – Buxton road, and for most of its length is across expanses of wild, treeless and often bleak moorland, which looks uninviting and menacing in poor, especially misty, weather. But on a fine day the attractions of such a lovely open landscape are manifest: unimpeded sweeping views in all directions, a remoteness and solitude broken only by the sound of the wind rustling through the heather and cotton grass or the sound of running water, and an exhilarating feeling of spaciousness and freedom. The half-way point is Three Shire Heads, a beautiful spot where not only do streams and paths meet, at a pack-horse bridge, but the counties of Cheshire, Staffordshire and Derbyshire also converge. There are short sections of rough walking and some modest climbing. Unless experienced with a compass, save this walk for good weather.*

At 1,690 ft (507 m) the Cat and Fiddle is the second highest inn in England, beaten only by the Tan Hill Inn in the northern Pennines. It was built to serve the new turnpike road completed in 1823, which was later superseded by the present A537 Macclesfield – Buxton

Pannier's Pool below the pack-horse bridge – a secluded setting where three counties meet

road. Not surprisingly it is a popular haven for walkers, cyclists and motorists alike.

With your back to the inn, take the track opposite (public bridle-way sign to Danebower) across open moorland. As the walk starts from such a high altitude there are immediately impressive views, looking south-westwards towards Shutlingsloe and Wildboarclough. Drop down through Danebower Hollow, and after 1½ miles (2·25 km) you reach the A54 **(A)**. Turn right for about 100 yards (92 m) and then turn sharp left along a track (almost doubling back), go through a gate and turn right again by the side of a chimney, heading steeply downhill towards the River Dane. Pick up a grassy track, turn right, climb a stile and, keeping by the river on the left, go through several gates and over stiles, past ruined quarry buildings, for one mile (1·5 km) to Three Shire Heads **(B)**. This is a lovely spot, the meeting place of two streams, crossed by two pack-horse bridges, in a setting of narrow, steep-sided, fern-covered valleys, with rocks and falls and even some trees – a rarity in this wild and open landscape. It is also where the county boundaries of Cheshire, Staffordshire and Derbyshire meet – hence its name. Just below the main pack-horse bridge is Panniers Pool; panniers were the large baskets carried by pack-horses, and the pool was probably used either as a ford, before the bridge was built, or as a drinking place for the horses.

Turn left over the first bridge, at a public bridle-way sign, go through a gate and continue by a stream on the right. Keep ahead through another gate to a junction of paths and continue along an uphill tarmac track which, after a right-hand junction, becomes a rougher track across the lonely,

bleak moorland. Before the track ends, fork up left across rough grassland (no discernible path at this stage), to a wall corner. Climb two stiles in quick succession and bear right, now picking up a recognisable path again and following it up to the road at Dane Head (**C**). Turn right for a few yards and then turn left, at a public footpath sign to Goyt valley, along a broad grassy path over the bleak expanses of Axe Edge Moor. This rises to over 1,800 ft (540 m) and ends at the abrupt gritstone escarpment of Axe Edge, overlooking Buxton and a good slice of the Peak District. It is a major watershed and five rivers (Dove, Manifold, Wye, Derwent and Goyt) begin

their journey to the sea from its watery slopes.

Just before a brow ahead, turn left along a much narrower grassy path which soon bears right down to a road (**D**). Cross over, keep ahead across rough grass for a few yards and then turn left onto a clear path and follow it, by a broken wall on the right, to a lane. From here there are fine views to the right looking towards the Goyt valley, and the Cat and Fiddle can be seen on the ridge ahead. Continue along the lane, turning left at a T-junction to follow it uphill back to the starting point.

18 Beresford and Wolfscote Dales

Start:	Hartington
Distance:	8 miles (12·75 km)
Approximate time:	4½ hours
Parking:	Hartington
Refreshments:	Pubs and cafés in Hartington, pub and café in Alstonefield
Ordnance Survey maps:	Landranger 119 (Buxton, Matlock & Dovedale) and Outdoor Leisure 24 (The Peak District – White Peak area)

General description *North of Dovedale proper the River Dove flows through the narrow and steep-sided Wolfscote and Beresford Dales before broadening out as it approaches Hartington. Many claim that these dales are just as attractive as the lower and more popular (and therefore certainly more crowded) part of Dovedale. All such claims are, of course, a matter of personal taste, but by any standards this is a superlatively beautiful walk which includes two of the loveliest Peak District villages, one on the Derbyshire side and the other on the Staffordshire side of the Dove; outstanding sweeping views from the higher points, and some long stretches of glorious riverside walking through the dales themselves.*

Like a number of Peak District villages, Hartington was once a market town, and the limestone houses, inns and shops grouped attractively around the spacious Market Place, with a duckpond to one side of it, create the atmosphere and impression more of a town than a village. It lies in a grand setting, about ½ mile (0·8 km) from the river, where the Dove valley widens out to the north of Beresford Dale, and is dominated by its large and handsome medieval church.

From the Market Place, take the road to Warslow and in a few yards turn left, by the public conveniences, at a public footpath sign to Beresford Dale. Go through a gate and bear right, keeping by a wall on the right, to a stile. Climb over, cross a walled lane, climb the stone stile opposite and continue across a field. There are lovely views ahead of the Dove valley and, beyond that, the Manifold valley: a lush, gentle, wooded landscape. The winding path is well waymarked and heads down to a stone stile by a gate, then continues up and down again to another stile. Climb it and keep ahead along a path which now becomes wider and better surfaced and continues through trees to join the banks of the River Dove. Now follow the river through the wooded Beresford Dale for nearly ½ mile (0·8 km). The whole of this area is associated with the famous angler Izaak Walton, who published *The Compleat Angler* in 1676. He frequently fished this part of the river, in the company of his friend Charles Cotton, who lived at nearby Beresford Hall. The hall was demolished in 1858 but the seventeenth-century Fishing Temple still survives.

Turn right over a footbridge by Pike Pool, so called by Charles Cotton, not after the fish, but after the thin spire of rock which towers above the river here. Continue along the other bank to another footbridge. Do not cross it but turn right along a lane **(A)**, and after fifty yards (46 m) turn left over a stone stile by a gate and along the edge of a field, by a wall on the right. Climb another stile, keep ahead, skirting the base of a hill on the left, and go through a succession of gates and stiles, along the path that curves gently left into the dry valley of Narrowdale.

At a meeting of paths turn right **(B)** along a walled path up to Narrowdale Farm, turn left between the farm buildings, go through a gate and continue climbing steadily, keeping by a wall on the left. Past a stone stile in the wall on the left, the path bears slightly right away from the wall, along a grassy ledge high above the dale, to another stone stile. Climb it and continue by a wall on the right, over a series of stiles, skirting the left-hand edge of a small group of trees and heading across fields to a lane **(C)**.

Turn left along the lane into Alstonefield, a delightfully unspoilt and peaceful village standing 900 ft (274 m) up on a plateau between the Dove and Manifold valleys. Its grey stone cottages are grouped around a charming green, complete with village inn, and the lovely old church is reached down a lane leading off from the green. Although

The picturesque village of Alstonefield

mostly fourteenth- and fifteenth-century, the church retains a Norman doorway and chancel arch, and it still contains the family pew formerly used by the Cottons from nearby Beresford Hall.

In the village centre bear left, following signs to Lode Mill and Ashbourne, and at the second public footpath sign on the left, turn off onto a straight walled track **(D)**. The track later bears right and left and continues as a narrower walled path to a stile. Climb over and bear right to drop down steeply, with lovely views ahead, to the River Dove.

Cross Coldeaton Bridge and turn left **(E)** to follow the river for 2¼ miles (3·5 km) along a most delightful path through Wolfscote Dale. The journey through Wolfscote Dale is the highlight of the walk: steep and thickly-wooded at first, and later more open, with lovely smooth grassy slopes and spectacular limestone crags.

By a footbridge and National Trust sign, turn right along an uphill path **(F)**, cross a path junction and keep ahead along a walled track. Where the track bends right, continue over a stone stile and across a field, bearing slightly right to some stone steps in a wall. Climb over and turn left along a lane. Soon after the lane curves to the right, turn left, at a public footpath sign for Hartington, along another walled track which soon turns sharply right and then keeps in a straight line to a narrow lane **(G)**. Turn left along this lane and follow it for about ¾ mile (1 km), finally dropping down into Hartington, with a grand view ahead of the church dominating the village below it. At the main road turn left back to the Market Place.

SCALE: 1:25 000 or 2½ INCHES to 1 MILE

19 Ilam and Dovedale

Start:	Dovedale
Distance:	8½ miles (13·5 km)
Approximate time:	4½ hours
Parking:	Car park at southern end of Dovedale
Refreshments:	Tea-room at Ilam Hall, café at Milldale
Ordnance Survey maps:	Landranger 119 (Buxton, Matlock & Dovedale) and Outdoor Leisure 24 (The Peak District – White Peak area)

General description *It is no wonder that so many visitors have enthused about Dovedale over the centuries, for by any standards it is supremely beautiful, one of the loveliest valleys in England. Indeed, Dovedale is sometimes a victim of its own beauty, becoming overburdened with visitors, especially on summer Sundays and Bank Holidays. The consequent problems of footpath erosion mean a constant battle for the National Trust, who own most of the area. But at a quiet time – a fine weekday in spring, autumn or even winter – this is a magical walk, across fields to the model estate village of Ilam and through the grounds of Ilam Hall by the Manifold, followed by a climb up to Stanshope, and a descent, with superb views, into the valley of the Dove at the hamlet of Milldale. Finally comes the enchanting walk downstream along the winding river, through the limestone ravine of Dovedale itself – an unforgettable experience.*

From Dovedale car park climb a stile on the opposite side of the road, at a footpath sign to Ilam, turn left along a broad track for a few yards and then bear right up steps to a double stile. Climb over, passing the Izaak Walton Hotel on the left, keep ahead over two stiles and bear slightly left across the next field to a gate. Go through, continue to another stile, climb over, and bearing left off the main path head down to a gate and onto a road. Turn right into Ilam.

Ilam is basically the creation of one man, Jesse Watts Russell, a wealthy industrialist, owner of the hall, who imitated some of his aristocratic contemporaries by remodelling his estate; not only rebuilding the hall but also resiting the village. He rebuilt Ilam Hall in

The entrance to Dovedale

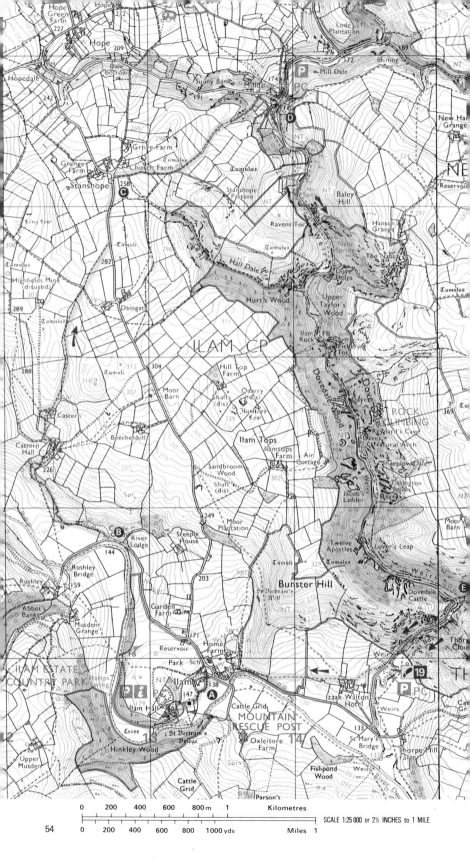

SCALE 1:25 000 or 2½ INCHES to 1 MILE

the Gothic style in the 1820s, and built the new village in the 1850s, out of sight of the hall, in a picturesque Alpine style unique in the Peak District. The imitation Eleanor Cross was in memory of his wife. He also restored the small thirteenth-century church, adding the octagonal and rather over-proportioned memorial chapel to his father-in-law. The church is noted for its Saxon treasures: a font in the church and two crosses in the churchyard. It also contains the tomb of St Bertram, a little known eighth-century Mercian saint.

Turn right at the Memorial Cross (A), and where the road bends right keep ahead for a few yards; bear left along a path (signposted 'Church') and, passing to the right of the church, continue up to the hall. Ilam Hall was partially demolished in the 1930s but what was left of it was given by Sir Robert McDougall, along with large areas of Dovedale, to the National Trust, who lease part of the hall to the Youth Hostels Association and also have an information centre and shop there.

Proceed across the terraced garden, from where there is a marvellous view of the hall and church in the foreground and, beyond, of Bunster Hill and Thorpe Cloud guarding the entrance to Dovedale. Pass through a gate in the far left-hand corner of the garden and turn right along the path that heads down through trees towards the river, turning right again on reaching the riverside path to join the Paradise Walk. Soon you come to the 'Battle Stone', the shaft of an eleventh-century cross discovered in the foundations of a cottage during the rebuilding of Ilam. It is so called through being popularly associated with local battles between the Anglo-Saxons and Vikings. Climb a stile, keep ahead to a metal stile, climb that and continue, now by the banks of the River Manifold (sometimes a dry river-bed at this stage). Keep along a delightful wooded path, go over three stiles and finally through a gate onto the road by River Lodge. The last part of this path is across a private garden, for the use of which you will be charged the princely sum of one penny.

Turn left and where the road curves to the left keep ahead along a tarmac track (B); this winds and climbs steadily up to the fine old house of Castern Hall, bends left around the edge of the house and then right at a public footpath sign to Stanshope, continuing up towards a farm. Turn left through a gate at a public footpath sign, continue to a gap in the wall ahead, go through and turn right by the wall. From here there is a superb view up the Manifold valley. At a public footpath sign turn right, and keeping to the left of the farm buildings head towards another public footpath sign, turning left over a metal stile

by a gate. Bear half right and keep ahead across rough grass, making for some stone steps in a wall on the right. Climb over, turn left, and keeping by a wall on the left walk along the edge of a series of fields, climbing five stiles. After the last one, bear left across a field to a stone stile, climb over and continue ahead, clipping the right-hand side of a wall corner and bearing right to a stile and public footpath sign.

Climb over and turn left along the road into the hamlet of Stanshope. At a left-hand bend, turn right, at a public footpath sign to Milldale, along a walled track (C). Where the track bears right, keep ahead through a gap by the side of a gate, at a public footpath sign, and go along the edge of a field by a wall on the left. In front there are lovely views looking towards Dovedale. Go through a gate, continue by a wall on the right, pass through a gap at the side of the next gate and keep ahead, with the tower of Alstonefield Church crowning the skyline to the left. Climb two stone stiles and continue down the valley (which grows steeper and narrower all the time), through a gap in a wall by a cottage and ahead to a lane. Here turn right into the idyllic hamlet of Milldale, which is perched on the western banks of the Dove. The National Trust has an Information Barn here, next to Viator's Bridge, which gives some of the history of Milldale.

Cross the picturesque Viator's Bridge, a narrow two-arched bridge referred to by Izaak Walton and Charles Cotton in The Compleat Angler, turn right (D) through a gate and follow the popular, well constructed path, which keeps by the river for over 2½ miles (4 km). This takes you through the beautiful, steep-sided, well wooded Dovedale, which is overhung with a series of limestone crags, caves and pinnacles. Among the outstanding features passed on this delightful and dramatic walk are, in order: Ravens Tor on the right, the caves of Dove Holes on the left, the twin pinnacles of Ilam Rock on the right (by a footbridge) and Pickering Tor on the left, the great yawning gap of Reynards Cave on the left, Jacob's Ladder on the right and Tissington Spires on the left. Then the route climbs via steps to Lover's Leap, a rocky outcrop and superb viewpoint, before descending to the river again and passing the crag of Dovedale Castle on the right.

Soon the distinctive shape of Thorpe Cloud comes into view. On reaching the Stepping Stones over the Dove (E), either cross them and turn left along the other bank of the river, or continue ahead for about ¼ mile (0·4 km), and then turn right over a footbridge and left along the other bank. Either way it is about ½ mile (0·8 km) from the Stepping Stones back to the car park.

20 Baslow and Curbar Edges

Start:	Baslow
Distance:	7 miles (11·25 km)
Approximate time:	3½ hours
Parking:	Baslow
Refreshments:	Pubs and cafés in Baslow, Chequers Inn near Froggatt, pub at Calver
Ordnance Survey maps:	Landranger 119 (Buxton, Matlock & Dovedale) and Outdoor Leisure 24 (The Peak District – White Peak area)

General description *A magnificent gritstone escarpment stretches along the eastern rim of the Derwent valley, from Birchen Edge northwards to Derwent Edge, providing both exhilarating walking and glorious views. This walk traverses Baslow Edge and Curbar Edge, two of the finest sections of this long escarpment, before plunging through thick woods to the banks of the Derwent and returning along the river-bank and across fields to Baslow. There are two ascents, the longer one being at the beginning to take the walker onto the edges.*

Looking over the Derwent valley from the gritstone boulders on Curbar Edge

The rather suburbanised and strung-out village of Baslow lies at the northern end of Chatsworth Park and near the southern limit of the long line of gritstone edges, occupying a frontier position on the River Derwent between the limestone of the White Peak and the gritstone of the Dark Peak. From the car park cross the main road and take the uphill road opposite (Eaton Hill). At a T-junction turn right along Bar Road **(A)**. Past the last houses, the road degenerates into a rough track which continues climbing, following public footpath signs to Baslow and Curbar Edges, bearing right and left and heading up to a gate. Go through and keep ahead to the top of the ridge, from where the Wellington Monument can be seen just over to the right. This was erected in memory of the Duke of Wellington in 1866, and on the opposite side of the valley stands a twin monument to Nelson.

Before reaching the monument, turn left **(B)** and head towards a huge solitary boulder called the Eagle Stone. Now comes a most exhilarating walk across breezy, open, heathery moorland, following the top of Baslow Edge. Approaching a lane, go through a gate, cross the lane, keep ahead to go through another gate and continue across Curbar Edge – another superb walk across more spacious, heathery moorland, passing impressive rocks and crags and with magnificent views across the Derwent valley to the left.

At the point where a wall on the right joins the path, bear left off the path, along a ledge in front of the face of the crags ahead. About half-way across this face, turn sharp left **(C)** down a steep, narrow, rocky path which immediately plunges into the thick woodland that clothes the hillside. Soon the path begins to level out, continuing through the woods to a ladder stile. Climb over and keep ahead to a road. Cross over (the Chequers Inn is just to the right), climb a stone stile opposite and continue across a field, through a broad gap in the trees, to another stile. Climb over, continue ahead for a few yards, climb a stone stile onto a lane and turn right down to Froggatt Bridge.

Cross the bridge and turn left over a stone stile **(D)** along the riverside path by the Derwent, initially through conifer woods and later by delightful tree-fringed meadows (with good views of the edges on the skyline to the left), as far as the road by New Bridge **(E)**. Cross the road and continue along a track opposite, at a public footpath sign to Calver Bridge, through woods, over a stile, and across more meadows, this time a little further away from the river. Climb a stile by a farm and continue along a track into Calver.

At the road turn left over Calver Bridge, catching a glimpse of the fine, early

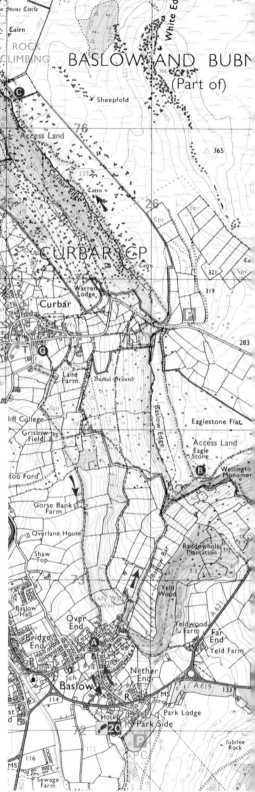

nineteenth-century Calver Mill, whose forbidding appearance made it a suitable substitute for Colditz Castle in the television series. On the other side of the bridge take the middle of three roads **(F)**, by the side of a church, following it steeply uphill for just under ½ mile (0·8 km) into Curbar. At a crossroads **(G)** turn right along a lane signposted to Cliff Cottage, and just after a right-hand bend turn left over a stone stile, at a public footpath sign to Baslow via Gorse Bank Farm. Follow a path, first between a wall and hedge and then along the edge of a field, to a stone stile in front of a farm.

Climb the stile and turn right along a walled path to another stone stile. Climb that and continue by a wall on the left to a ladder stile. Turn left over it and keep ahead, by a wall on the right, to a gate. Go through, head across the middle of a field up to another gate, pass through that and turn right through yet another gate. Continue across a field to a fourth gate, go through that and keep ahead, by a wall on the right, to a stone stile. Climb over and bear left across a narrow field to some steps and a stone stile at its corner.

Climb over, keep ahead along a broad track, go through a gate and past Gorse Bank Farm, continuing along the track for ½ mile (0·8 km) to the edge of Baslow, where the track becomes a tarmac road leading to a T-junction. Turn right and first left **(A)** down Eaton Hill back to the starting point.

SCALE 1:25 000 or 2½ INCHES to 1 MILE

21 Derwent Edge

Start:	Fairholmes car park and picnic area near the Derwent Dam
Distance:	7 miles (11·25 km)
Approximate time:	3½ hours
Parking:	Fairholmes car park
Refreshments:	Café at car park
Ordnance Survey maps:	Landranger 110 (Sheffield & Huddersfield) and Outdoor Leisure 1 (The Peak District – Dark Peak area)

General description *From just below the massive wall of the Derwent Dam, the walk proceeds along the track by the shores of the Derwent Reservoir and then climbs across fresh and bracing moorland to the prominent outcrop of Back Tor on Derwent Edge. Then follows a superb scenic walk along the edge, from where many of the best-known landmarks in the Peak District can be picked out, before the route descends to the banks of the Ladybower Reservoir. Although the construction of reservoirs, building of dams and planting of conifers on the lower slopes of the surrounding hills have created an artificial landscape in the upper Derwent valley, it is nevertheless a very attractive and possibly even an enhanced one.*

SCALE 1:25 000 or 2½ INCHES to 1 MILE

Towards the end of the nineteenth century, regular water supplies were required for the large cities of Derby, Nottingham, Leicester and Sheffield, which encircle the Peak District, and the upper Derwent valley seemed ideal for the construction of reservoirs: sparsely populated, relatively narrow (making the building of dams easier) and with a high rainfall. Subsequently a chain of three reservoirs was built — Howden, Derwent and Ladybower — creating one of the largest man-made areas of water in Europe.

Leave the car park and turn sharp right down a lane that passes in front of the Derwent Dam. Because of the geographical similarities between the Derwent Reservoir and those in the Ruhr, it was used for the practice runs for the famous 'Dambusters' raid on Germany in 1943, and also used as the setting for the film. At the west side of the dam is a memorial to all those who died in the raid.

Where the lane curves to the right, turn left (A) along an uphill path through conifer plantations, climbing past the side of the dam wall and continuing alongside the reservoir. Climb a stile and turn left along a rough road that runs by the reservoir. From here the views through the trees across the water to the dam wall, the plantations on the other side and the distant moorlands beyond are as impressive as those across any natural lake.

Just where the track starts to curve gently to the left, turn right (B) onto a path which heads through the trees, by a stream on the right, climbing up to join a wall on the right. Leaving the trees, continue straight ahead, climbing steeply between grass and ferns to a public footpath sign to Strines via Bradfield Gate Head. Keep ahead across open grassland and heathery moorland up to a ladder stile and another public footpath sign. Climb over and continue (in the direction of Strines) across a lovely, fresh, wilderness landscape with splendid panoramic views across Derwent Reservoir to the Derwent and Howden Moors and, to the right, down Ladybower Reservoir to the Ashopton Viaduct. The grassy path flattens out for a while, then bears right to start climbing again, continuing ahead (ignore a path to the left) and bearing right to the prominent cairn and view indicator on the summit of Lost Lad

(C). This rocky outcrop is named after a young shepherd boy who died from exposure near here, having carved the words 'lost lad' on a boulder. Keep ahead into a dip and up again to the trig. point on the summit of Back Tor (D) just a short distance in front, another superb viewpoint.

Now turn right for a splendid walk along Derwent Edge, the most northerly of the long line of gritstone edges along the eastern side of the Derwent valley. In a short while you reach a public footpath sign at Bradfield Gate. From here continue straight ahead along the edge, with superb views all the time, passing a series of spectacular rock formations: Cakes of Bread, Dove Stones (flat, upturned slabs), Salt Cellar (very aptly named), White Tor and finally the prominent and very impressive Wheel Stones, also called the Coach and Horses.

Continue past the Wheel Stones to a path junction and public footpath sign (E). Here turn right in the direction of Derwent and start to descend, bearing right on meeting a wall and keeping by that wall on the left to another public footpath sign. Bear left through a gap in the wall along a grassy path, heading for the right-hand edge of a plantation. Go through a gate and continue between a wall and the plantation fence down to another gate. Pass through that and go along a path, by a wall on the left, to yet another gate. Go through, cross a stream and keep ahead to a stile. Climb over, keep around the edge of a barn on the left to a gate, go through and continue downhill, bearing right and dropping down across a field to a stile in the far corner.

Climb over and turn right along the track by the Ladybower Reservoir (F) to a footbridge over Mill Brook. Beneath the waters of the reservoir at this point lies the submerged village of Derwent, drowned in 1943, when the waters of the reservoir rose.

Continue along the track, which soon becomes a tarmac lane, by the side of the reservoir, for a pleasant and relaxing walk of one mile (1·5 km), finally following the lane round to the left in front of the Derwent Dam and back to Fairholmes car park.

Derwent Reservoir — its artificiality diminished by time, trees and a moorland setting

22 Marsden and Standedge

Start:	Marsden
Distance:	8 miles (12·75 km)
Approximate time:	4 hours
Parking:	Parking area at top of Station Road by canal
Refreshments:	Pubs and cafés in Marsden, Junction Inn near entrance to Standedge Tunnel
Ordnance Survey maps:	Landranger 110 (Sheffield & Huddersfield) and Pathfinders 702 (Huddersfield & Marsden) and 714 (Holmfirth & Saddleworth Moor)

General description *Where does the Peak District end and the Pennine range begin? That is an impossible question to answer as they merge imperceptibly into each other, but this merging must take place somewhere in the vicinity of Marsden. Though on the northern fringes of the Peak District National Park, both the towns and the scenery in this area are unmistakably Pennine in atmosphere and appearance. This walk is mostly across open, bare moorland; bleak perhaps but impressive, and characterised by sweeping and uninterrupted vistas. It is obviously best appreciated on a fine, clear day, when walking will also be much easier and pleasanter. There are no strenuous climbs, but mud is likely to be an ever present problem, particularly along that section which utilises a part of the Pennine Way over Marsden Moor.*

The buildings of Marsden climb up the steep hillsides near the head of the Colne valley. It is very much a Yorkshire woollen town; small and not unattractive with some imposing-looking mills. From the parking area turn left and follow the tow-path of the Huddersfield Narrow Canal for ½ mile (0·8 km) to the canal basin at Tunnel End. Here begins the Standedge Tunnel, at just over 3 miles (4·75 km), the longest canal tunnel in Britain, and one of the greatest constructional feats of the Industrial Revolution. It was completed in 1811 and was closed in 1944. It was a 'legging' tunnel, which means that the boatman lay on his back and propelled the barge by pushing with his legs against the tunnel roof. The row of cottages near the tunnel entrance has now been converted into an information centre.

Cross the canal just before the tunnel entrance **(A)**, bearing right up a lane to the Junction Inn. Here keep ahead along Waters Road for about ¾ mile (1 km), through the hamlet of Hey Green, and by the entrance to Hey Green Hotel keep ahead for a few yards **(B)** and then bear left, at a public footpath sign to Willykay Clough, through a gate and along a path by a stream on the left. Cross the stream by an old pack-horse bridge, turn right by a beck on the right, cross another beck and turn left, at a footpath sign for 'Packhorse Road', going up through a shallow clough, by a beck on the left, and onto the open expanses of Marsden Moor.

The wild bare moorland looks endless as you follow a waymarked path, lined with posts, for 1½ miles (2·25 km) to a road. A few yards before the road, turn sharp left onto the Pennine Way **(C)** and keep along that across more open moorland. The combination of the tramping of thousands of feet and badly-drained, peaty soil ensures that this section of the route is likely to be muddy at any time of the year, even after a prolonged drought (and there are not too many of those up on this Pennine – Peak District fringe country). On seeing some reservoirs ahead bear left, following a series of cairns, along the top of Standedge, a line of crags from which there are fine and

extensive views across the valley to Saddleworth Moor. *Stan* was the Saxon word for stone, and Standedge therefore means simply an edge lined with stones.

Continue past the trig. point, over two stiles and ahead to a gap in a wall. Go through, turn right to climb a stile about 50 yards (46 m) ahead and keep ahead, dropping down and turning left on meeting a broad track to a road **(D)**. Cross over to the car park opposite and, at a Pennine Way sign, turn left along a path which squeezes between the road on the left and wire fence on the right, in the direction of Redbrook Reservoir. Keep along a path to the right of the reservoir, from which there are sweeping views over the smooth, bare slopes of Wessenden and Meltham Moors and, beyond the reservoir, the distinctive conical shape of Pule Hill. Continue along the path past the reservoir, dropping down and then up a steep clough just before reaching a road, near a junction **(E)**.

At this junction take the narrower left-hand fork and in a few yards bear slightly left, at a public footpath sign, along a broad track that runs above and parallel with the narrow lane. At this point there are three parallel routes leading back to Marsden: a road, a lane and this track, and from the track there are some impressive views of Butterley Reservoir to the right, and Marsden lying near the head of its narrow valley ahead. Keep along the track to a path junction, go through a gate and turn right downhill, keeping ahead over a stile at a public footpath sign, and continuing down a grassy path to a gap in a wall by the next footpath sign. Turn right, keeping by a wall on the left, pass through another gate and turn left downhill to a stream. Cross the stream and continue along the uphill path in front, which curves gradually to the right and passes through a broken wall. Keep ahead along the edge of a field, following it round to the left to the far corner by a group of trees.

Here climb a stile, keep ahead for a few yards and then turn right down a track to a lane. Turn left down to the main road, cross over and continue ahead along Towngate, by the church wall on the left, finally turning left up Station Road to the starting point.

23 Bakewell, Chatsworth Park and the River Wye

Start:	Bakewell
Distance:	9 miles (14·25 km). 8 miles (12·75 km) if detour to Haddon Hall is omitted
Approximate time:	5 hours (4 ½ hours for slightly shorter version)
Parking:	Bakewell
Refreshments:	Pubs and cafés in Bakewell, café in Edensor, tea-rooms at both Chatsworth House and Haddon Hall
Ordnance Survey maps:	Landranger 119 (Buxton, Matlock & Dovedale) and Outdoor Leisure 24 (The Peak District – White Peak area)

General description *As well as its limestone dales, gritstone moors and lovely villages and towns, the Peak District is renowned for its great houses, two of the finest of which, Chatsworth and Haddon, are passed on this walk. The walk also includes two particularly attractive stretches of riverside, woodland, meadows, and glorious views (especially while climbing between the Wye and Derwent valleys), and it starts and finishes in a most pleasant and interesting old town.*

Bakewell's intriguing blend of building styles, from the sixteenth to the nineteenth centuries, is a reflection of its varied roles as an ancient market town, short-lived spa, minor textile town and, more recently, an important tourist centre.

Bakewell puddings, the well known local delicacy, are supposed to have originated around 1860 as the result of an error made by a cook in one of the town's hotels. When asked to make a strawberry tart, he apparently put the jam in first and poured the egg mixture over it, instead of the other way round.

Start at the Market Place and walk down to the picturesque fourteenth-century stone bridge over the Wye. Turn right into Station Road and follow it as it curves left uphill. Take the first road on the right **(A)** and, by the last house, turn right along a path at a public bridle-way sign to Ballcross. Continue ahead, entering woodland and climbing steadily all the while. At the far end of the woods turn right along a lane, from which there are fine and extensive views as it starts to descend into the Derwent valley. At a junction, bear right along a rough, unmade road **(B)** and continue downhill through an avenue of trees into the village of Edensor.

Edensor is a purpose-built estate village which was constructed here by the sixth Duke of Devonshire between 1838 and 1842, because the original village, which it replaced, spoilt the view over the park from Chatsworth House.

Walk through the village, past the church and through some white gates onto a road. Cross over and continue along the path straight ahead, making for the group of trees on the brow of a hill. From here comes the first breathtaking view of Chatsworth, probably the finest view of all — the magnificent, palatial residence surrounded by its sweeping parkland, set against a glorious backcloth of wooded hills, and with the waters of the Derwent below, crossed by an

SCALE 1:25 000 or 2½ INCHES to 1 MILE

elegant eighteenth-century bridge.

Continue down to the bridge, and if visiting the house cross it and proceed up the drive; otherwise turn right just before the bridge along the riverside path **(C)**. Chatsworth was built between 1686 and 1707 for William Cavendish, first Duke of Devonshire, on a scale befitting the main residence of one of the most prominent aristocratic families in the kingdom. Inside, the rooms are sumptuous, and a tour of these includes the suite of state rooms, baroque chapel, painted hall, oak room (with superb wood carvings) and magnificent library. In the early nineteenth century a new north wing was built, including an orangery, dining room, music gallery and sculpture gallery. The gardens in the immediate vicinity of the

The incomparable setting of Chatsworth

junction. Here bear left along a broad bridle-way, keep to the right at the next path junction and continue heading downhill.

At the next public bridle-way sign, where the main track swings to the left into a farmyard, keep ahead for about 200 yards (184 m) and then turn right through a gate. Keeping by some iron railings on the left, continue downhill, passing through two gates and bearing left to go through a third gate, and turn sharp left along a wide track. Follow this winding downhill track to the river **(F)**.

Here there is a choice of either heading straight back to Bakewell or making a short and very worthwhile detour of just over one mile (1·5 km) to visit Haddon Hall. If continuing to Bakewell, pick up the route at point (F) below.

For the visit to Haddon, turn left over a stile, at a public footpath sign to Haddon Hall, and follow a riverside path, eventually crossing the Wye and continuing up to the main road. The entrance to Haddon Hall is about 200 yards (184 m) along the road to the left.

The contrasts between Chatsworth and Haddon are immediately obvious. Whereas the former is grand, formal and classical, the latter is smaller, more informal and irregular. Whereas Chatsworth is surrounded by sweeping landscaped parkland, Haddon possesses a series of intimate terraced gardens that rise above the river. Haddon Hall is basically a late medieval manor house which came into the possession of the dukes of Rutland. Because it was not their main residence, they did little to modernise or extend it, which explains its largely unaltered appearance and unspoilt charm and authenticity. The main rooms are built around a paved courtyard, and particularly noteworthy are the panelled banqueting hall (complete with minstrels' gallery), medieval chapel and the marvellous light and airy long gallery, with a beautifully decorated plaster ceiling.

Return to the bridge over the Wye to resume the walk back to Bakewell **(F)**. At a public footpath sign to Coombs Road, go through a gate and follow a well waymarked path ahead across a field, keeping roughly parallel to the winding river. Climb a stile, later on cross a footbridge, and continue ahead. Climb another stile and keep ahead to pass through a gate and along a track by an arm of the river up to a footbridge. Turn left over the bridge and head across a field to another bridge which crosses the main channel of the Wye. Cross it and turn right to follow the river up to the medieval bridge, turning left back to the town centre.

house are formal; originally laid out in the seventeenth century, they were added to in the nineteenth by Joseph Paxton, who also built the huge 290 ft Emperor Fountain in honour of a visit by the Czar of Russia that never materialised. Beyond the formal gardens is the park, redesigned in the eighteenth century by the renowned landscape architect 'Capability' Brown, who created the sweeping lawns and random groups of trees, and even straightened the river. The moving of Edensor to its present site in the nineteenth century completed the process. Neither man nor nature was allowed to stand in the way of the grand design that the dukes wanted.

Continue for the next mile (1·5 km) along the riverside path through Chatsworth Park, a delightful walk across meadows with constantly changing views across the Derwent to the great house and wooded slopes behind it. Just past a weir, bear right by a ruined building and through a white gate onto a road **(D)**. Turn left and then bear half right to cross a car park, pass through the gate at the far end and continue along the lane ahead, bearing right into the hamlet of Calton Lees. Turn sharp left at a T-junction, and at the end of the buildings climb a stone stile ahead and turn left along a path signposted to Rowsley. Soon the path meets a wall on the left and follows it as far as a stile. Turn left over it, then turn right and continue through several gates and across fields to rejoin the River Derwent. Keep by the river to Rowsley, bearing slightly right to a gate and stile. Climb over, continue to another stile, climb that and keep ahead, at first by a wall on the right and later along a broad track, under a railway bridge to a lane **(E)**.

Turn right along the lane and follow it uphill, under another railway bridge and past the church. Soon the lane narrows to a rough track, signposted to Bakewell, and continues through most attractive woodland to the top of the hill, with superb views over both the Derwent valley behind and the Wye valley in front. At a junction of paths keep ahead to descend, by a wall on the left, to a T-

24 Macclesfield Forest and the 'Cheshire Matterhorn'

Start:	Clough House car park, just to the north of Wildboarclough
Distance:	8½ miles (13·5 km)
Approximate time:	5 hours
Parking:	Clough House car park
Refreshments:	None
Ordnance Survey maps:	Landranger 118 (Stoke-on-Trent & Macclesfield) and Outdoor Leisure 24 (The Peak District – White Peak area)

General description From a distance, particularly, it is easy to see why Shutlingsloe has been described as the 'Cheshire Matterhorn', for its abrupt and distinctive peak, although only rising to 1,659 ft

(498 m), does bear a striking resemblance to its somewhat higher Continental counterpart. Much of this walk is across the former royal hunting ground of Macclesfield Forest, a sparsely-populated area of isolated farms, rolling hills, wild and open moorlands and rushing streams. The area has seen little change over the centuries apart from the planting of conifers and construction of reservoirs on its western perimeter, both of which features provide pleasant walking and, in this instance, add to rather than detract from the landscape. For most of the way this is an undulating walk but towards the end there is a long, though not particularly steep or strenuous, climb to the summit of Shutlingsloe, followed by a short, sharp descent.

Macclesfield Forest comprises a number of plantations occupying the western slopes of the Peak District and overlooking the Cheshire Plain, and is just a small part of what was, in the Middle Ages, a large royal hunting forest. Much of it would have been, as today, open moorland rather than thick woodland.

Turn right out of the car park and walk

Macclesfield Forest

along the lane for one mile (1·5 km). Just after passing the turning to Forest Chapel on the left, turn right onto a farm track (**A**), cross a stream, turn left through a metal gate and keep along a broad path by Clough Brook on the left. Passing the left-hand side of a farm, turn left through a gate down to the brook, cross a footbridge and turn right. Keep by a wall on the right to a field corner and turn left uphill (**B**), passing a ruined farm building on the left. Walk up some steps ahead (just past the ruined farm), climb a stile, turn right, by a wall and fence on the right, for fifty yards (46 m) and then turn left along a grassy path, through a shallow depression, keeping ahead to a wall. From

here there are fine views of Shining Tor on the right and Shutlingsloe on the left.

Climb some stone steps and continue by a wall on the left, turning left over a ladder stile in that wall and heading across a field to a gate. Go through, turn right and follow the edge of a field, by a wall on the right, down to a metal gate. Pass through it, continue through a farmyard and bear right down to a lane (**C**). Turn left and immediately bear right at a junction, along a lane signposted to Forest Chapel. After about 100 yards (92 m) turn right (at a 'No Vehicles' sign) along an enclosed uphill track to Macclesfield Forest Chapel, less than ½ mile (0·8 km) away. This plain and simple church, built in 1673 and

SCALE 1:25 000 or 2½ INCHES to 1 MILE

reconstructed in 1831, is in total harmony with its surroundings, and from it there are fine views over the wild and open forest landscape. It is one of a number of churches where a rushbearing ceremony is held to commemorate the annual renewal of the rushes which originally covered most church floors.

Continue past the chapel, turn right along a stony path, and just before reaching the edge of the trees, by a public footpath sign to Walker Barn, bear left off the track (**D**) and climb a stile to enter the forest. Follow a waymarked path through the dense woodland, a pleasant mixture of conifers and hardwoods on a steeply sloping hillside, for ¾ mile (1 km) to a path junction (**E**). This path can become very muddy and slippery in wet weather.

Here turn left (sign: Langley) and continue downhill through the forest, emerging into more open country where, on the right, there is a superb view of Tegg's Nose ridge and the reservoir below it. Just before a lane and gate ahead, turn left over a stile and turn right along the lane. Follow it to a junction and, at a public footpath sign, turn left over a stile (**F**) along a path that runs just below the embankment of Ridgegate Reservoir. At a public footpath sign, turn left over a stile and along a path through trees, soon joining the side of the reservoir. Turn right up some steps, at a yellow waymark, along a forest track, turning left at the next yellow waymark and continuing along to a stile, between trees on the left and a wire fence on the right.

Climb the stile, keep ahead along the lane for a few yards and shortly afterwards bear right over a stile (**G**), at a footpath sign to Shutlingsloe, along a path through the trees, at first by a wire fence on the left and keeping roughly parallel with the lane. The well waymarked path proceeds to another footpath sign. Here turn right (sign: Shutlingsloe) along a broad uphill track through the forest. Where the track forks near a more open area, take the right fork and continue up through dense woodland. At the top edge of the trees, bear slightly right away from the track to a stile, climb over and continue, now across open moorland with stunning views all round, still climbing steadily. Over the brow Shutlingsloe is suddenly seen, now just a short distance ahead. Continue along a clear path towards it, with a final brief but steep climb to its summit (**H**).

From here there unfolds a magnificent panorama that includes Macclesfield Forest, Tegg's Nose, the Cheshire Plain, Axe Edge, Tittesworth Reservoir, Roach End and Mow Cop. Bear left from the summit, steeply downhill, along a waymarked path, following the path across a field towards a farm. At a public footpath sign keep ahead to a stile, climb over, continue down to another stile, climb that and turn right, soon bearing left by a wall on the left to a farm track.

Bear right along the track, from where there is a fine view of the imposing Crag Hall ahead, and on meeting the boundary wall of a wood turn sharp left (**J**), keeping by the side of that wall. Pass a cottage on the left and, with fine views over to the right across the valley of Clough Brook and the moors beyond, continue along a grassy path, by a wall on the left and keeping by the edge of trees on the right. Climb two stiles, eventually reaching a lane by a ladder stile. Turn right over the stile and turn left along the lane for the short distance back to the car park.

25 Eyam, Bretton Clough and Eyam Moor

Start:	Eyam
Distance:	9½ miles (15·25 km)
Approximate time:	4½ hours
Parking:	Eyam
Refreshments:	Pubs and cafés in Eyam, pub in Foolow, Barrow Inn at Bretton Mount
Ordnance Survey maps:	Landranger 119 (Buxton, Matlock & Dovedale) and Outdoor Leisure 24 (The Peak District – White Peak area)

General description Not only is the plague village of Eyam a fascinating place in itself, it also lies amidst outstandingly attractive countryside. The walk starts by taking field paths to Foolow, then climbs up to Eyam Edge and drops down through the lovely wooded valley of Bretton Clough. It continues along the valley of Highlow Brook and climbs back over the heathery expanses of Eyam Moor before returning to Eyam village. This lengthy walk embraces deep wooded valleys, open moorland, and magnificent views all the way, but perhaps its strongest appeal lies in the heroic story of Eyam itself, during the plague years of 1665 and 1666.

In September 1665, when the Great Plague was at its height in London, George Viccars, a tailor lodging in the cottage of Mary Cooper in Eyam, died of a strange fever. He was the first of Eyam's plague victims and by the time

the plague ended a year later, over 260 lives, out of a total population of around 350, had been lost, and whole families had been wiped out. According to tradition George Viccars himself was responsible for introducing the plague germs into Eyam, in cloth that he had ordered from London. As the plague spread like wildfire through the small village community, the villagers, under the courageous leadership of their vicar, William Mompesson, and his predecessor Thomas Stanley, voluntarily cut themselves off from the outside world in order to stop the infection spreading. Food and medical supplies were left at various points on the boundary of the village, the church was closed and services suspended, and families buried their own dead near their homes. Today there are many poignant reminders of those terrible events in the village: the Plague

Cottage by the church (where George Viccars lodged with Mary Cooper and the first death occurred), the numerous family graves scattered all over the immediate area, the boundary stone and Mompesson's Well on the edge of the village, where supplies were left to be collected, and in the churchyard the grave of Catherine Mompesson, the vicar's wife, who died on 25 August 1666.

Leaving aside this single traumatic event which had such a profound effect on the village and made such a lasting impression on the rest of the country, Eyam is a most interesting and attractive village with handsome stone cottages lining its long main street and a fine mainly fourteenth-century church. There is a Saxon font in the church, a well preserved Saxon cross in the churchyard and, as well as all the sad reminders of the plague, there is the unusual grave of a Derbyshire cricketer, Harry Bagshaw, showing a wicket being hit by a ball and the raised finger of the umpire, indicating that his innings was over.

Turn left out of the car park down to the main street and turn right past the ruins of Bradshaw Hall on the right, which at one time was used as a cotton mill. Turn sharp left into Tideswell Lane and walk past houses, looking out for a yellow waymark by a short flight of steps on the right (**A**). Here turn up the steps and along a narrow path to a stone stile. Climb over and head in a virtually straight line for nearly 1½ miles (2·25 km) to Foolow. The path is easy to follow, crosses a number of fields and climbs over innumerable stone stiles. On the right, below the wooded slopes of Eyam Edge, can be seen Black Hole Mine, and this, along with Furness Quarry on the left, is a reminder of the former industrial importance of this area. Approaching Foolow the path bears right to a road, where you turn left into this most picturesque village. Its stone cottages, pub and tiny church are grouped around the village green and pond, and there is a medieval cross in the middle of the green, where it was placed in 1868.

In the village centre turn right (**B**) along the lane to Bretton for just under ½ mile (0·8 km). At a public footpath sign, turn left over a stone stile, bear right along the edge of a field, by a wall on the right, climb another stone stile and keep ahead to some steps and a stile. Climb up and over and keep ahead through fern, ascending the ridge to a crossroads of paths just in front of the next stile (**C**). Turn right along a narrow path to rejoin the lane.

Turn left uphill and follow the lane to the top of the ridge, from where the views are extensive, and keep ahead to the Barrel Inn, which has stood on this site since at least the

Plague Cottage, at Eyam

seventeenth century. Turn left along a tarmac track **(D)**, between the inn and a cottage, and follow it downhill. In front there are superb views of Bretton Clough, the village of Abney and the hills beyond. Soon after passing a farm on the left, the track bears right. At this point keep ahead along a narrow walled path to a stile. Climb over and continue, by a wall on the left, along the edge of a field down to another stile. Climb that and bear slightly left to descend towards the wooded, steep-sided Bretton Clough. The path turns right, drops steeply, then turns sharply left into the trees and sharp right again to a stile. Climb over and continue ahead along a delightful path through fern, grass and trees, keeping along the right-hand side of the clough. At a ruined building, keep to the left of it, go through a broken wall down to a stream and continue ahead, eventually reaching the footbridge at Stoke Ford after a most attractive walk through the clough of over a mile (1·5 km).

Do not cross the footbridge but turn right **(E)** along an uphill path above the valley of Highlow Brook on the left. The path keeps along the edge of the valley, first climbing high above it and then dropping down into woods to join the brook near a stile. Climb over and continue through pine woods to a gate. Go through and keep ahead along the edge of a field, following a grassy path through several gaps in walls, eventually passing through a gate and along a track to a lane. From here the views over the Derwent valley, the village of Hathersage and the long line of gritstone edges are magnificent.

On reaching the lane, turn sharp right **(F)** and follow it uphill, as it bends left and right again, for ½ mile (0·8 km) as far as a public footpath sign to Sir William's Road, on the right opposite a farm. Here turn right over a stone stile and then turn left along a clear, fairly straight path across the heather and fern of Eyam Moor, with grand views over the Derwent valley on the left, for one mile (1·5 km). Climb a stile onto a lane **(G)** and turn right along Sir William's Road, a broad walled track that was once part of a turnpike road, allegedly named after Sir William Cavendish though there are other local 'Sir Williams' who could be candidates. Follow this for ½ mile (0·8 km) before turning left over a ladder stile at a public footpath sign **(H)**. Continue along the edge of a field, by a wall on the left, to drop down to a stone stile and a lane **(J)**. In front the fine view of Eyam in the valley below is somewhat marred by the Furness Quarry.

Turn left along the lane for a few yards and turn right at a public footpath sign, over a stile, and head diagonally across a field to another stile. Climb that, keep ahead to another one, climb that and continue along the boundary wall of a wood on the right to yet another stile. Climb it and turn right at a public footpath sign, heading steeply downhill and bearing left through trees, by a wall on the right, to a stile. Climb over and continue down steps to a lane **(K)**. Cross over, climb the stone stile almost opposite and continue along the edge of a field, by a wall on the right, down to a stone stile in a wall corner. Climb it and keep along the edge of the next field, by a wall on the left, to another stone stile. Climb that and continue along a path that leads down to the boundary wall of Eyam churchyard. Pass through a metal gate and walk through the churchyard to the main street. Turn right, passing the Plague Cottage and the fine seventeenth-century facade of Eyam Hall on the right, and turn right again back to the car park.

26 Lathkill Dale

Start:	Monyash
Distance:	10 miles (16 km). Shorter version 8½ miles (13·5 km)
Approximate time:	5 hours (4 hours for shorter version)
Parking:	Monyash
Refreshments:	Pubs and cafés in Monyash, pub and café in Over Haddon
Ordnance Survey maps:	Landranger 119 (Buxton, Matlock & Dovedale) and Outdoor Leisure 24 (The Peak District – White Peak area)

General description The Derbyshire Dales are famed for their outstanding beauty and by any criteria Lathkill Dale is one of the loveliest, as this walk so richly demonstrates. Starting from the pleasant village of Monyash the route heads across mostly open country, briefly dropping into the dale and out of it again to the village of Over Haddon. It soon drops down into the dale again at Conksbury Bridge, to be followed by a superlatively beautiful three-mile (4·75 km) ramble along the steep-sided, wooded banks of the Lathkill, undoubtedly the highlight of the walk. Finally it climbs through the gorge at the head of the dale before returning to Monyash. Although it is a lengthy walk, there is very little climbing involved.

Monyash, a farming and former lead-mining village, is situated high on the limestone uplands near the head of Lathkill Dale. The base of the fourteenth-century market cross on the village green, and a fine mainly fourteenth-century church with spire and transepts, are the main clues to its importance from medieval times as a market and route centre.

Start by turning right along Chapel Street and first left at the old cross along the wide main street. Turn right over a stile by the side of a gate to go through the churchyard, climb another stile at the far end and keep ahead along a track to join a lane. Turn left along this lane for fifty yards (46 m) and, where it bends right, keep ahead along a broad track, at a public footpath sign marked Limestone Way, and continue ahead at a second public footpath sign (Lathkill Dale) along a walled track.

The track gives extensive views all around and you follow it as far as a stone stile beside a metal gate. Climb over and continue by a wall on the right, shortly climbing a stone stile in that wall and heading across, at a

The pure waters of the Lathkill at Conksbury Bridge

public footpath sign to Cales Dale, to another stone stile at a public footpath sign to Youlgreave. Climb over, continue by a wall on the left, go over a stile and ahead to yet another stone stile in the wall, just before reaching the end of the field. Turn left over it and right along the edge of a field, this time with the wall on the right, heading gradually downhill to a metal gate on the right. Go through and keep ahead along a broad track down to One Ash Grange Farm. As the name indicates, this was once a grange; it was owned by Roche Abbey near Rotherham, and the well known Victorian Quaker and reformer, John Bright, spent his honeymoon here (Monyash being a centre of the Quaker movement at that time).

Walk through the farmyard and bear left, following footpath signs and yellow waymarks, to a flight of steps by the side of a barn. Go down them and keep ahead, climbing another stile, to descend the wooded slopes of Cales Dale. The path drops through a gorge, and at a Limestone Way sign turns sharp right down to a stile **(A)**. Climb that and head steeply up the other side of the dale along a stepped path, emerging at the top to climb a stile and continue across a field in front. From here there is a superb view behind and to the left, of Cales Dale and its junction with Upper Lathkill Dale. The path follows convenient yellow waymarks, heading in a straight line for the middle of a line of trees on the horizon. Follow a footpath sign to a gate in the wall that borders the trees. Go through and head across to a stile, climb over that, bear right along the edge of a field to a gate, go through that and continue across the next field, making for the far corner near another belt of trees.

Here climb a stile and keep ahead by a wall on the left for a few yards, before bearing slightly right to another stile. Climb that and continue along a clear path across the middle of a large field, bearing right at a footpath sign to a stile. Climb over, keep ahead a few yards to another stile, climb that, and keeping parallel to a wall on the left head for a stone stile and footpath sign. After climbing over, turn left along a road **(B)** for about ½ mile (0·8 km), and at the bottom of a dip turn left over a stone stile at a public footpath sign **(C)**, heading straight across a field in the direction of Over Haddon, clearly seen ahead. All around are grand, wide views over the Wye and Derwent valleys across a typical Peak District landscape.

Climb a stile and keep ahead at a public footpath sign to another stile, climb that and continue in the same direction, following waymarks to a wall corner. Bear left to follow the wall and go through a gate, continuing

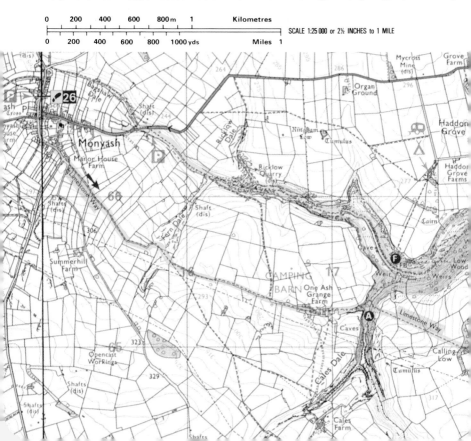

SCALE 1:25 000 or 2½ INCHES to 1 MILE

straight ahead through a farm. In the next field bear slightly right, heading towards some trees near the top right-hand corner, and pass through a gate to enter the Lathkill Dale National Nature Reserve. Head down through the trees, bearing sharp left to cross a footbridge over the river **(D)**.

Here you can shorten the walk slightly by turning left along the path through Lathkill Dale and omitting the Over Haddon 'loop'. The extra distance of 1¾ miles (2·5 km) is worth while, however, for three reasons: an attractive village, grand views and a fine old bridge.

Keep ahead along the uphill lane into Over Haddon, a remote, rural village which, from its 800 ft (244 m) elevation, enjoys striking views across Lathkill Dale and the valleys of the Wye and Derwent beyond. Its present tranquillity belies the fact that it was once a lead-mining settlement, like many other similarly sleepy Peakland villages. Walk past the church, bear right at a junction through the village and, just before a chapel, bear right again, passing the Lathkill Hotel on the left, to a stone stile and public footpath sign to Alport. Climb over and bear right across a field, from where there are the most outstanding views over the steep, wooded dale below, with the buildings and church-tower of Youlgreave and rolling hills behind. Head for a wall corner, bear left along a ledge above the Lathkill, climb a stile and head across a field, gradually bearing right all the time to drop down steeply to another stile. Climb that and continue down to the road just above Conksbury Bridge.

Walk down the road and just before the bridge turn sharp right along the riverside path **(E)**. Now comes a splendid and exceptionally attractive three-mile (4·75 km) walk through Lathkill Dale, keeping by the river all the while. As you proceed up the beautifully wooded dale, both the river and the dale become narrower and the dale gets steeper. At a footbridge bear right, rejoining the previous route for just a few yards **(D)**, and then turn left to continue along the riverside path. The Lathkill is a very pure and clean river. Sometimes its progress is impeded by vegetation, so that it flows in a series of separate channels, sometimes it flows as a single stream; sometimes it is fast-flowing over rocks and at others its waters are still and calm. Further up the dale it sometimes drops over weirs and falls, and at times it even disappears underground.

On emerging from the trees, at the junction of Lathkill and Cales Dales by a footbridge, keep ahead **(F)**, still on the same side of the river, which has now narrowed considerably, towards the head of the dale. Climb a stile and continue through an increasingly narrow and steep-sided limestone gorge, eventually arriving at the top of the dale. Climb another stile and continue along a grassy path, going over a third stile and ahead to a road. Here turn left to follow it back to Monyash.

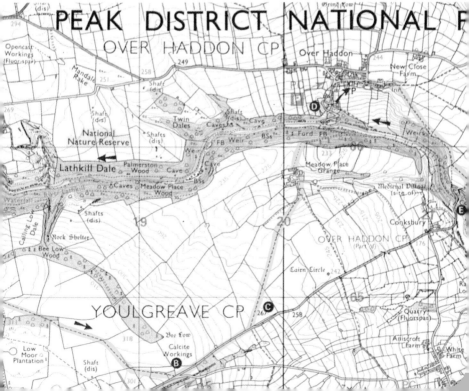

27 The Roaches and Lud's Church

Start:	The Roaches
Distance:	9 miles (14·25 km). Shorter version 5 miles (8 km)
Approximate time:	4 ½ hours (2 ½ hours for shorter version)
Parking:	Roadside parking area at the Roaches just to the north of Upper Hulme
Refreshments:	None
Ordnance Survey maps:	Landranger 118 (Stoke-on-Trent & Macclesfield) and 119 (Buxton, Matlock & Dovedale), Outdoor Leisure 24 (The Peak District – White Peak area)

General description *The gritstone edge of the Roaches forms the dramatic western boundary of the Peak District, looking across the lowlands of Staffordshire and Cheshire. It is a fascinating area of weirdly contorted rocks which, together with Back Forest to the north, provides a magnificent ridge walk of over three miles (4·75 km). To the east, in the thick woodlands of Forest and Gradbach Woods, the equally fascinating, even menacing, deep and secluded chasm of Lud's Church, with its links with medieval religious heresy, is visited. All this creates a spectacular and absorbing walk which, though fairly lengthy, is only moderately strenuous, and a shorter alternative can be followed if desired.*

Go through the gate beside the parking area and bear right along the path between the distinctive, conical-shaped Hen-Cloud on the right and the Roaches on the left. The name Roaches probably comes from the French word 'roche' meaning rock. Approaching the base of the rocks, turn left at a footpath sign along a path parallel to them, and after passing Rockhall Cottage turn right through a gap in the wall and take the path ahead, which ascends through the strange-looking rock formations, bearing right to climb some steps in the rock face. Turn left and walk through a quite incredible landscape of contorted rocks lying about at random, amidst trees and above steep slopes, with fine views to the left over a contrastingly gentle countryside, from which Tittesworth Reservoir stands out prominently.

At a footpath sign, turn right up onto the ridge itself and turn left along the top **(A)** for a splendid ridge walk that gives magnificent views on both sides. Soon the small, quiet, mysterious-looking Doxey Pool is passed on the right, and the path continues to the trig. point which marks the 1,658 ft (497 m) summit of the Roaches. Now the path starts to drop down, with a particularly striking view of Shutlingsloe ahead, past Bearstone Rock to the lane at Roach End **(B)**.

*Here the route can be shortened by taking the path on the right, and in a few yards the longer route is rejoined at **(D)** by a stone stile and footpath sign.*

Cross the lane, climb some steps and two stiles in quick succession and continue by a

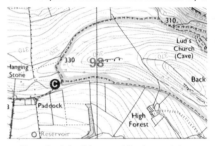

wall on the left. After a while the path leaves the wall, and now comes another fine ridge walk, this time along Back Forest, smoother, lower, and with fewer rocky outcrops than the Roaches. After 1 ¼ miles (2 km) the path descends to a signpost and path junction **(C)**. Here turn right following a footpath sign to Gradbach along a pleasant sunken path, amidst fern, heather and bilberries, which keeps by a wall on the left.

The path curves right into Forest Wood, and at a junction of paths by a rocky outcrop on the left you take the right-hand fork, following the sign to Lud's Church. Continue through the woods and in a short while turn right off the path, through a cleft in the rocks and down some steps on the left, to enter the damp, narrow, secluded, perpendicular chasm called Lud's Church, whose sides are covered with fern and moss and above which the trees look rather precariously perched on the rocks. It is alleged that this inaccessible spot was a meeting place for Lollards, a group of heretics, followers of John Wycliff, who were prominent in the fourteenth and fifteenth centuries. Persecution and the constant threat of execution by burning forced them to meet in secret hideouts, and this place would certainly have been eminently suitable. It is supposed to derive its name from one of these Lollards, called Walter de Ludank.

Continue to the far end of the chasm and climb up out of it, bearing right up steps and squeezing through the sheer narrow sides, up more steps and along a path ahead, which after a while bears left to rejoin the main path. Here bear right and continue through Forest Wood, bearing right at a footpath sign to Roach End to climb out of the wood and proceed ahead along a paved path, keeping by a wall on the left. Look out for a stone stile in that wall by a footpath sign, climb it and turn sharp left **(D)** down a farm track, here rejoining the shorter route.

Walk past the farm and keep ahead along a grassy track that bears right across open moorland, gradually descending into the valley of Black Brook. Cross the brook, bear right to a stile by a footpath sign, climb over and keep ahead, following the brook through the quiet and lonely valley, whose sides are clothed with fern, heather and random groups of trees. Passing a farm on the right, climb a stile next to a gate at the end of the farm buildings, turn left and then right over a footbridge, and pass through another farm, this time with the farmhouse on the left. Now take a walled track ahead, climb a stile and continue by a wall. Where that wall ends, keep ahead by a fence to a stile on the right, climb it and continue by a ditch on the right, later crossing it and following the other side of it along a walled track (though the walls are virtually ruined), up to a stile.

Climb over and turn right along an uphill lane, taking the first turn on the right. With excellent views of both the Roaches and Hen Cloud ahead, follow this lane, bearing right at the next junction, for ½ mile (0·8 km). At the first farm track on the left **(E)**, turn left over a cattle-grid and follow the broad track across bare and open moorland, gradually heading uphill. Where the track forks, take the right-hand one up to a stile by a gate. Climb over, keep ahead towards a metal gate, and just before reaching it, climb a stile in the fence on the right. Continue ahead, keeping by a wall on the left, over a slight brow, from where there is a fine view ahead of Tittesworth Reservoir. The path heads in its direction, through the gap between the Roaches and Hen Cloud. Keep by a wall on the left, finally dropping down to the lane by the parking area.

SCALE 1:25 000 or 2½ INCHES to 1 MILE

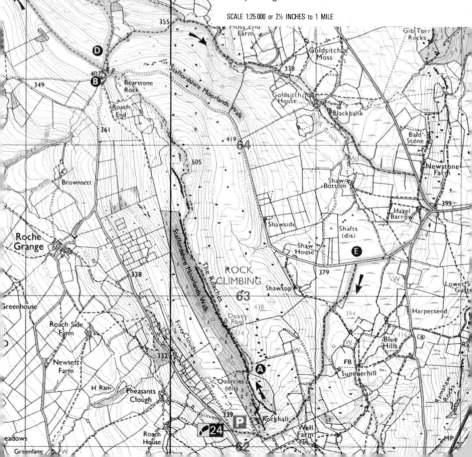

28 Edale and Jacob's Ladder

Start:	Edale
Distance:	7½ miles (12 km)
Approximate time:	4 hours
Parking:	Edale
Refreshments:	Pubs and cafés in Edale
Ordnance Survey maps:	Landranger 110 (Sheffield & Huddersfield) and Outdoor Leisure 1 (The Peak District – Dark Peak area)

General description *This walk starts at the village of Edale and follows the first few miles of the Pennine Way up the rocky and steep Grindsbrook Clough, climbing onto the lower slopes of Kinder Scout at the head of Edale. There is a sense of the wilderness about the next stage as the route follows the head of the dale round – with magnificent and widely contrasting views all the way – and passes some fantastically shaped gritstone boulders, before dropping down via the well known Jacob's Ladder for an easy final stretch back to the starting point. Part of* the walk is across open, featureless moorland that presents few route-finding difficulties in clear conditions, but in bad weather and especially when visibility is poor you should definitely not attempt it unless an experienced walker able to use a compass.

Strictly speaking Edale is the name of a valley rather than a single settlement, a collective name for five nearby hamlets or booths. In practice it has become particularly identified with Grindsbrook Booth, because that is the main settlement where the church for the whole parish is situated. Northwards stretches the highest and wildest moorland of the Dark Peak, and Edale has become a major walking centre, its two inns, youth hostel, guest-houses, farms and cafés providing the last taste of civilised living for intrepid walkers before they tackle the rigours of the 250 mile (400 km) Pennine Way. This modest walk by comparison only follows the first 2 miles (3 km) of it.

From the car park turn right up the lane through Grindsbrook Booth, past Edale church, and straight ahead where the lane becomes a rough track. Bear right at a Pennine Way sign along a narrow path down through trees **(A)**, go over a footbridge, up the steps ahead and bear left along a broad path that follows the side of Grindsbrook Clough. Pass through a gate, keep ahead

0	200	400	600	800 m	1		Kilometres		
0	200	400	600	800	1000 yds		Miles	1	

SCALE 1:25 000 or 2½ INCHES to 1 MILE

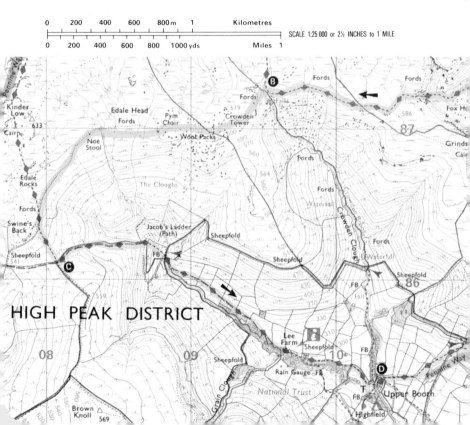

through trees, go through another gate at the far end of the small plantation and bear left over a stream. To the right is the wild and narrow valley of Golden Clough, rising steeply to high moorland.

Continue along the side of the valley, which now becomes more rugged and open, and the path starts to ascend, fairly gently to begin with but later becoming steeper, rougher and rockier. Cross the stream and continue along the other side of it through the increasingly narrow valley, picking your way through boulders and climbing to a cairn at the top, avoiding a left fork through a gorge. From here continue straight ahead across the bare, open, high moorland with superb panoramic views, the bleak slopes of Kinder Scout and the moors ahead contrasting vividly with the gentler and lusher scenery of the vale of Edale. The path traverses soft, black peat, and despite the lack of landmarks is easy to follow as it cuts a black swathe across the moor (its bareness relieved somewhat by a scattering of cotton grass), passing rocky outcrops and dotted with cairns along the way. There is a lonely, top-of-the-world feeling upon these quiet open moors, with no sound except that of the wind, which is hardly ever absent.

At the head of the steep narrow valley of Crowden Clough on the left **(B)**, the route leaves the Pennine Way, which turns right here, and continues across a rocky stream, turning left and climbing steeply up the side of the valley to the superb vantage point of Crowden Tower, the first of a series of

Grindsbrook Clough — first stage of the Pennine Way

impressively large and fantastically shaped gritstone outcrops passed during the next ¾ mile (1 km). Continue along a path, which is still quite clear, across a number of deep peat gulleys (called groughs), passing in succession: the Wool Packs (a very large group of rocks), Pagoda Rocks (so named because one of them resembles a Chinese pagoda), Pym Chair (on its own, a little to the right, looking like a seat) and the distinctive Noe Stool (anvil-shaped and near a large cairn). Here the path starts to curve gently to the left around the head of Edale, with more magnificent views down the dale, passing more cairns and heading downhill to a stile, gate and meeting of paths.

Turn left down the right-hand edge of the valley to another path junction **(C)**. Turn left again, soon bending right to descend Jacob's Ladder, part of a pack-horse trail from Hayfield to Edale where the pack-horse trains dropped down by a series of steps into the valley below. At the bottom cross a stream, go through a gate and keep ahead along a straight, clear, well surfaced path, through several stiles and gates, and past Lee Farm, finally crossing a stream into the tiny hamlet of Upper Booth **(D)**.

Turn left through Upper Booth Farm, turn right through a gate, and following public footpath signs to Edale keep along the fairly straight route ahead, which alternates between a rough track and a grassy path, over a series of stiles, skirting the base of Grindslow Knoll. Finally bear left, at a public footpath sign to Edale in the middle of a field, to a stile by some trees. Climb over, turn right along a sunken path lined with trees and hedges, climb another stile and go through a gate into Grindsbrook Booth. Turn right to retrace your steps through the village back to the car park.

Useful Organisations

The Countryside Commission,
John Dower House, Crescent Place,
Cheltenham, Gloucestershire GL50 3RA.
Tel: 0242 21381

The National Trust,
36 Queen Anne's Gate, London SW1H
9AS. Tel: 01-222 9251 (East Midlands
Regional Office, Clumber Park
Stableyard, Worksop, Nottinghamshire
S80 3BE. Tel: 0909 486411)

Council for National Parks,
45 Shelton Street, London WC2H 9HS.
Tel: 01-240 3603

The Peak National Park Office,
Aldern House, Baslow Road, Bakewell,
Derbyshire DE4 1AE. Tel: 062 981 4321

National Park Authority Information Centres
can be found at:
Bakewell	(Tel: 062981 3227)
Castleton	(Tel: 0433 20679)
Edale	(Tel: 0433 70207)
Fairholmes	(no telephone)
Torside	(no telephone)
Hartington	(no telephone)

East Midlands Tourist Board,
Exchequergate, Lincoln LN2 1PZ.
Tel: 0522 31521

Peak and Northern Footpaths Society,
1 Nelson Street, Hazel Grove, Stockport
SK7 4LR. Tel: 061 483 2482

The Ramblers' Association,
1/5 Wandsworth Road, London
SW8 2LJ. Tel: 01-582 6878

The Forestry Commission,
Information Branch,
231 Corstorphine Road,
Edinburgh EH12 7AT.
Tel: 031 334 0303

The Youth Hostels Association,
Trevelyan House, 8 St Stephen's Hill,
St Albans, Hertfordshire AL1 2DY.
Tel: 0727 55215

The Long Distance Walkers' Association,
Lodgefield Cottage, High Street,
Flimwell, Wadhurst, East Sussex
TN5 7PH. Tel: 058 087 341

The Council for the Protection of Rural
England,
4 Hobart Place, London SW1W 0HY.
Tel: 01-235 5959

Ordnance Survey,
Romsey Road, Maybush, Southampton
SO9 4DH. Tel: (0703) 792764/5 or
792749

Ordnance Survey maps of the Peak District

The Peak District is covered by Ordnance
Survey 1:50 000 (1¼ inches to 1 mile)
Landranger map sheets 109, 110, 118 and
119. These all-purpose maps are packed with
information to help you explore the area.
Viewpoints, picnic sites, places of interest,
caravan and camping sites are shown, as well
as public rights of way information such as
footpaths and bridle-ways.

The Peak District area is also covered by an
Ordnance Survey Tourist map at 1 inch to 1
mile scale.

To examine the area in more detail, es-
pecially if you are planning walks, Ordnance
Survey Outdoor Leisure maps at 1:25 000
(2½ inches to 1 mile) scale are ideal. Two
Outdoor Leisure maps cover the Peak
District:

Sheet 1 — The Peak District . —
Dark Peak area
Sheet 24 — The Peak District —
White Peak area

Areas not available in the Outdoor Leisure
map series are instead covered by Pathfinder
maps. Also at 1:25 000 (2½ inches to 1 mile),
these are the perfect maps for walkers.

To look at the area surrounding the Peak
District, Ordnance Survey Routemaster maps
at 1:250 000 (1 inch to 4 miles) scale will
prove most useful. Sheets 5 (Northern
England) and 6 (East Midlands) are relevant.

Ordnance Survey maps and guides are
available from most booksellers, stationers
and newsagents.

Index